Classics

WIGAN

RUGBY LEAGUE FOOTBALL CLUB

Dean Bell, who has written the foreword for this book, was a key member of the great Wigan side of the late 1980s and early 1990s. The outstanding New Zealand centre was the club captain for three seasons, during which he led his side to a trio of Wembley successes. Here he proudly displays the Challenge Cup after the second win – over Widnes in 1993.

Classics
WIGAN
RUGBY LEAGUE FOOTBALL CLUB

GRAHAM MORRIS

TEMPUS

Martin Offiah covers his face at Wembley in 1994 as he contemplates having scored possibly the finest individual try seen at the stadium.

Front cover illustration: Wembley joy in 1990 as Wigan, led by captain Ellery Hanley (behind trophy) and coach John Monie (wearing blazer), celebrate retaining the Challenge Cup after beating Warrington 36-14.

First published 2004

Tempus Publishing Limited
The Mill, Brimscombe Port,
Stroud, Gloucestershire, GL5 2QG
www.tempus-publishing.com

British Library Cataloguing in Publication Data.
A catalogue record for this book is available from the British Library.

ISBN 0 7524 3108 0

Typesetting and origination by Tempus Publishing Limited
Printed and bound in Great Britain

Introduction

This collection of fifty Wigan Classics is the second book from Tempus Publishing to chronicle a slice of the rich history of the Cherry and Whites. I use the word 'slice' because, having compiled the first Wigan title for Tempus in their Images of Sport series, I am well aware of the wonderful and success-laden past of this marvellous club. While that fact guarantees there is no shortage of material to put down in the pages that follow, it does (as I commented in the introduction to my previous effort) make it very difficult to determine what should end up on the 'cutting-room floor'. I am sure that, whichever fifty matches had made it into the final list, there would inevitably be many Wigan supporters who felt their own personal favourites had been excluded.

What do we mean by 'classic' matches? According to the dictionary, the word 'classic' relates to 'excellence' or a 'recognised masterpiece' and certainly many of Wigan's performances over the years would qualify for those accolades. I would argue, however, that in rugby terms, when supporters reminisce, 'classic' is a word often touted to describe all manner of games. Fans recall events that proved momentous in their minds not only for the quality of rugby that was on display but because of the occasion itself. In this category I would certainly place the Wigan versus Manly-Warringah world club decider at Central Park in 1987. It was a tough, uncompromising game without a try in sight, but it produced the kind of atmospheric evening that makes everyone who was in that 36,895 crowd proud to say 'I was there!' Similarly, there are games that have become a part of Wigan folklore: the excitement of the first touring side to appear at Central Park (New Zealand in 1907) and the demolition of the unfortunate Cumbrian amateurs Flimby and Fothergill in the 1925 Challenge Cup.

Many of the matches are, unashamedly, cup finals, often the highlight of any season, particularly if victory and silverware is the end result! It is certainly very difficult to ignore those great Wembley days; after all, there have been 22 featuring Wigan, 15 of which proved triumphant. The first, in 1929 against Dewsbury, was also the first Challenge Cup final taken to the famous stadium. It was not a classic confrontation, but it provided a magical day for Wigan and a proud moment in the career of the great Jim Sullivan. Wembley has since produced many true Rugby League classics, and two that fit the description admirably are Wigan's confrontation with Hunslet in 1965 and the match against Hull twenty years later. The former was every critic's 'best-ever' until the 1985 finale. If ever a Rugby League match was a 'recognised masterpiece' this was it! It had everything you could hope for; brilliant and skilful rugby, outstanding individual performances, great tries and a nail-biting finish.

There are many games recalled through pieces of individual prowess. Who can forget that wonderful length-of-the-field try when Martin Offiah brought the Wembley crowd to its feet in 1994? Again, it may be the subject of opinion as to whether this was a classic match, but it was most certainly a classic try. Two years earlier Offiah made headlines through scoring ten tries to annihilate the Wigan club record and an unfortunate Leeds outfit in a Premiership Trophy semi-final. Leeds were also on the receiving end when two other great wingmen, Mick Sullivan and Jason Robinson, scored never-to-be-forgotten tries to pull Wigan 'out of the fire' under tense circumstances. Sullivan's late effort put a Lewis Jones-inspired Leeds side out of the 1960 Challenge Cup, Robinson providing the winner in the defence-dominated first Super League Grand Final of 1998.

Some League matches that, otherwise, would not trouble the sports headlines too much can take on a far different significance when the wider picture is considered. Two such clashes took place in 1987 and 1991. The first, a one-sided 62-7 win over Featherstone Rovers, secured the Championship after a twenty-seven-year gap, turning the Central Park terraces into carnival mode throughout the second half! The second concluded what had been described as 'mission impossible' – Wigan winning at Leeds 20-8, in their eighth League match in a gruelling nineteen-day finale, to pip Widnes for the title by just two points.

When Wigan defeated Huddersfield in the 1950 championship decider without eight of their finest players (who were with the British tour party in Australia), it was described as the club's 'finest hour', but perhaps the greatest victory of all was achieved in Australia during June 1994. The outcome moved one eminent writer to describe it as 'one of the most outstanding achievements in the history of the British Rugby League.' I refer, of course, to the 20-14 World Club Challenge win over Brisbane Broncos, a highly creditable result that effectively earned them that year's BBC Sports Team of the Year award.

All of the matches referred to above find a place among the fifty featured, but I fully realise many worthy contenders have been omitted from this compilation. Hopefully, the final selection embraces some of the readers' own 'classic' moments.

Graham Morris
Worsley, May 2004

Wigan's 'finest hour', the 1950 Championship final victory over Huddersfield. Wigan's Bill Hudson – supported by Frank Barton (extreme left) – tackles Ike Owens.

Foreword
by Dean Bell

I'm a great believer that it is not so much what you achieve in life, but what you achieve with the ability that you have that matters. We have all got different levels of ability. I didn't have Martin Offiah's speed, Ellery Hanley's strength, Shaun Edwards' anticipation or Andy Gregory's skill, but I did have an unrelenting desire to get the best out of myself, which helped me achieve many things in the game of Rugby League. Without doubt another big factor was that I was privileged to play at one of the most famous clubs in the world alongside some of the greatest players that our game has ever seen. We had players with a lot of skill and talent, but we also had players who possessed the 'mental toughness' to win big games when the pressure was on.

The underlying memory of my first year was feeling how lucky I was to be surrounded by so many good players and thinking, 'I could be on to something pretty special here!' Winning so many trophies in the first year was great, although I have to be honest and admit that the one I really wanted, the Challenge Cup, eluded us. It devastated me so much when we lost to Oldham in 1987 that I will never forget that night. I think that was a big wake-up call for us for future games, in that we couldn't rest on our laurels. That match is famous for all the right reasons now because of what was to follow. In my mind, it was the catalyst for the future.

Ellery Hanley was a fine captain and obviously a very special talent, but the captaincy was something I always wanted. You want to go as far as you can and the Wigan club meant so much to me. My first Challenge Cup final as captain was against Castleford at Wembley in 1992. I remember feeling very anxious as I didn't want to be the first Wigan captain for many years to lose the Challenge Cup, most of all in a final. I felt both proud and relieved at the end of the game to go up first and lift the trophy.

What I looked forward to most about Wembley, apart from the experience of playing, was when you walk out of the tunnel and the explosion of noise and colour hits you. It is just a big adrenalin rush. I remember walking out to the halfway line to meet the dignitaries and it felt as though my feet weren't touching the ground! It was like floating, and I thought 'How good is this?' It is what I dreamt about as a youngster and now I was living the dream. One of the most precious things that will never leave me for the rest of my life is the homecoming after Wembley. It always made me feel so emotional because to me that's what the game is all about – the fans. It made me feel so humble that people had gone out of their way to decorate their homes and support us so passionately.

Central Park holds so many fantastic memories for me. We used to train on the top field behind the kop, and when we left the changing rooms the players used to go around the back. I was the only one, even if it was dark, who walked through the standing area on the kop. I remember Joe Lydon asking me one day, 'Why go that way?' I said, 'It's because every time I walk past I like looking at the pitch and thinking about the famous people that had been there prior to me.' I was keen to be part of that history. I used it to motivate myself and actually thought back about Billy Boston and other players strutting their stuff. The trophies and the memories are important, but what people remember is your effort and your character and that was what I was always trying to leave behind. No matter what the future holds for me, Wigan Rugby League Club has given me so many unforgettable memories, for which I am eternally grateful.

Dean Bell
Wigan Rugby League Club, May 2004

Acknowledgements

I am extremely grateful to the following individuals who have helped me in compiling material (images, match reports and statistics) for this book: Tony Collins (Rugby Football League), Ernie Day, John Edwards, Paul English, Mike Flynn, Robert Gate, Graham Gerrard, Michael Latham, Keith Mills, John Riding, Michael Turner, Brian Walker and Terry Williams (New South Wales Rugby League).

My sincere thanks go to the *Wigan Observer* (Philip Wilkinson in particular) for kindly agreeing to the inclusion of several photographs and match reports. Also, to *The Independent, Daily Telegraph* and *Yorkshire Post* for allowing me to reproduce match reports and to Topps UK Ltd for granting permission to reproduce their Merlin Trading Cards and Merlin Stickers. I would especially like to thank Micron Video Productions (particularly Phil Oakes) for patiently allowing me to review several 'modern' matches on film. Their help was invaluable.

My appreciation goes to staff at Manchester Central Library and Wigan Local History Library, both of which were most helpful during my research. I also acknowledge the work of Irvin Saxton and the Rugby League Record Keepers' Club and the excellent reference material contained in the Rothmans Rugby League Yearbooks (1981/82 to 1999, edited by Ray Fletcher and David Howes), League Publications Ltd's Yearbooks (1996 to 2002/03) and *They Played for Wigan* (Michael Latham and Robert Gate, 1992).

Last, but in no way least, special thanks to Dean Bell, who has contributed so much to the Wigan cause on and off the field and features prominently in the pages that follow, for so readily agreeing to write the foreword to this compilation.

List of 50 Matches

Date	Opponent	Venue	Competition
9 Nov 1907	v. New Zealand	at Central Park	Tour match
19 Dec 1908	v. Oldham	at Broughton	Lancashire Cup final
1 May 1909	v. Oldham	at Salford	Championship final
29 Mar 1913	v. Huddersfield	at Central Park	Challenge Cup round three
6 May 1922	v. Oldham	at Broughton	Championship final
12 Apr 1924	v. Oldham	at Rochdale	Challenge Cup final
14 Feb 1925	v. Flimby and Fothergill	at Central Park	Challenge Cup round one
8 May 1926	v. Warrington	at St Helens	Championship final
4 May 1929	v. Dewsbury	at Wembley	Challenge Cup final
28 Apr 1934	v. Salford	at Warrington	Championship final
4 May 1946	v. Wakefield Trinity	at Wembley	Challenge Cup final
18 May 1946	v. Huddersfield	at Maine Road, Manchester	Championship final
21 June 1947	v. Dewsbury	at Maine Road, Manchester	Championship final
22 Oct 1947	v. New Zealand	at Central Park	Tour match
1 May 1948	v. Bradford Northern	at Wembley	Challenge Cup final
20 Oct 1948	v. Australia	at Central Park	Tour match
13 May 1950	v. Huddersfield	at Maine Road, Manchester	Championship final
4 Nov 1950	v. Warrington	at Swinton	Lancashire Cup final
10 May 1952	v. Bradford Northern	at Leeds Road, Huddersfield	Championship final
10 May 1958	v. Workington Town	at Wembley	Challenge Cup final
27 Mar 1959	v. St Helens	at Central Park	League Championship
9 May 1959	v. Hull	at Wembley	Challenge Cup final
27 Feb 1960	v. Leeds	at Central Park	Challenge Cup round two
21 May 1960	v. Wakefield Trinity	at Odsal, Bradford	Championship final
8 May 1965	v. Hunslet	at Wembley	Challenge Cup final
22 May 1971	v. St Helens	at Swinton	Championship final
22 Jan 1983	v. Leeds	at Elland Road, Leeds	John Player Trophy final
4 May 1985	v. Hull	at Wembley	Challenge Cup final
12 Oct 1986	v. Australia	at Central Park	Tour match
5 Apr 1987	v. Featherstone Rovers	at Central Park	League Championship
7 Oct 1987	v. Manly-Warringah	at Central Park	World Club Challenge
30 Apr 1988	v. Halifax	at Wembley	Challenge Cup final
29 Apr 1989	v. St Helens	at Wembley	Challenge Cup final
10 Mar 1990	v. St Helens	at Old Trafford, Manchester	Challenge Cup semi-final
28 Apr 1990	v. Warrington	at Wembley	Challenge Cup final
13 Apr 1991	v. Leeds	at Headingley	League Championship
2 Oct 1991	v. Penrith Panthers	at Anfield, Liverpool	World Club Challenge
28 Mar 1992	v. Bradford Northern	at Burnden Park, Bolton	Challenge Cup semi-final
10 May 1992	v. Leeds	at Central Park	Premiership semi-final
17 May 1992	v. St Helens	at Old Trafford, Manchester	Premiership Trophy final
18 Oct 1992	v. St Helens	at St Helens	Lancashire Cup final
1 May 1993	v. Widnes	at Wembley	Challenge Cup final
30 Apr 1994	v. Leeds	at Wembley	Challenge Cup final
1 June 1994	v. Brisbane Broncos	at Brisbane	World Club Challenge
29 Apr 1995	v. Leeds	at Wembley	Challenge Cup final
21 May 1995	v. Leeds	at Old Trafford, Manchester	Premiership final
8 Sep 1996	v. St Helens	at Old Trafford, Manchester	Premiership final
28 Sep 1997	v. St Helens	at Old Trafford, Manchester	Premiership final
24 Oct 1998	v. Leeds	at Old Trafford, Manchester	Super League Grand Final
27 Apr 2002	v. St Helens	at Murrayfield	Challenge Cup final

WIGAN v. NEW ZEALAND tour match
9 November 1907, Central Park, Wigan

The first tourists to appear at Central Park were the 1907 New Zealanders, led by Hercules 'Bumper' Wright. A huge crowd greeted them at Wallgate Station as the train pulled in just after 11.30 a.m. on match day, having taken them from their Ilkley headquarters. Most were after a glimpse of Dally Messenger, the legendary Australian who was 'guesting' on the tour. Correctly anticipating a club record attendance, the gates opened earlier than usual, two hours before kick-off. Prior to the start, the visitors performed their now-familiar 'haka', the Wigan team responding with three cheers!

Following kick-off, proceedings were interrupted when supporters at the Greenough Street end surged through the rails onto the field. When play restarted, Wigan skipper Jim Leytham registered a brilliant individual try, kicking over the head of full-back Hubert 'Jum' Turtill to score in the corner, his attempted conversion being just wide. The visiting pack then started to win more of the ball and, following three failed goal attempts (two from Messenger, one by Edgar Wrigley), the New Zealanders finally scored, Wrigley going in at the corner. Messenger failed to add the extra points, leaving the sides level at 3-3 after 15 minutes' play. At this point, there was everything to play for, and both sides entertained the fans in what was described as 'a real ding-dong' with 'not a dull moment'. New Zealand were proving a handful, using short kicks to penetrate the Wigan defence and following up at speed. Wrigley came close to scoring tries twice before Wigan regained the initiative before half-time: Leytham raced around Turtill, having taken the ball at speed from a Bert Jenkins pass direct from a scrum, Tommy Thomas missing the goal.

With Leytham clearly a danger, the All Blacks opened the second half by withdrawing 'burly' forward Bill Tyler from the pack specifically to mark him. It failed to nullify the threat posed by the Wigan wingman who, having had what would have been a try-scoring pass to Jenkins intercepted by Turtill on the tourists' line and then hitting the post with a long-range penalty attempt, scored the try of the match. Receiving the ball just inside his own half, he beat three defenders in a touchline dash before being confronted once more by Turtill. This time he sprinted around his outside, managing to just keep inside the field of play, before placing the ball behind the posts to score and send the Central Park throng into raptures. Disappointingly, Thomas missed the goal, but the Cherry and Whites were now two

Wigan secretary George Taylor placed an advertisement in the local paper that offered reserved stand tickets at the princely sum of 4 shillings (20p).

The "All Blacks" Defeated.

TITANIC STRUGGLE AT CENTRAL PARK.

Brilliant Exhibition by the Wiganers.

"We are all very pleased to hear that the people of Wigan are taking such a keen interest in our visit this Saturday. Our desire all along has been to reach Wigan undefeated. If we are defeated—well, we will not be downhearted, for I am led to believe that it is no disgrace to be beaten on Central Park by the Cherry and Whites. New Zealand's flag, if it is struck, will not be lowered without a keen struggle."

These words formed the substance of a message which Mr. A. H. Baskerville, who organised the "All Blacks" tour, sent to the "Wigan Examiner" on Friday last, and which was read with the greatest interest by thousands of persons in Wigan and the surrounding districts. Since that communication was penned by Mr. Baskerville history has, without a doubt, been writ large in the sporting annals of the country—the first professional Rugby team from across the seas has entered the ancient borough with an unbeaten record, and what was regarded as the strongest contingent of "rugger" exponents which New Zealand can produce has departed shorn of its laurels. The events of last Saturday will live long in the memory of thousands, and in the decades which have yet to be the Titanic struggle which was waged on the banks of the historic river Douglas between the men from the home of the Maorilander and the chosen of Wigan will oft be the theme of conversation.

"ALL BLACKS" ARRIVAL.

The fact that the "Wigan Examiner" was able to announce the exact time of the arrival in Wigan of the New Zealanders led to a large number of the residents assembling in Wallgate shortly after ten o'clock on Saturday morning to witness the civic reception of the distinguished visitors. The officers of the Wigan Club were early in evidence on the platform of the Lancashire and Yorkshire Railway Station, and they were accompanied by several prominent citizens, amongst them being Mr. Sam Wood, J.P., the gentleman who was at noon to be elected Mayor of his native town. At 11-36, the time that the Yorkshire train was due in Wigan, the platform was crowded, whilst outside the station premises there was a throng of many thousand persons, the traffic having to be controlled by a large staff of police. As the train steamed into the station the New Zealanders were readily recognised, and ringing cheers were given as they stepped on to the platform and made their way to the exit. The men from the land of the fern, who had journeyed from their headquarters, The Spa Hydro, Ilkley, were first introduced to the new Chief Magistrate of the town, and then a move was made to the adjacent Victoria Hotel. The appearance of the New Zealanders in the main thoroughfare was the signal for another rousing cheer, and the men from "down under" were literally besieged by the crowd, which was naturally on the look-out for the "stars." Probably the most spoken of individual was Messenger. "Where's Messenger?" was the prevailing cry. "There's Messenger" and "There's Bumper Wright" were also repeatedly heard. Such is fame! However the Colonials had soon pushed their way into the hotel, where after further greetings had been extended the visitors partook of lunch, and subsequently settled down to enjoy a brief rest after their long journey from the Yorkshire coast.

The Inspiring War Cry.

Commencement of the Game.

A few minutes before three o'clock the respective teams lined up in the centre of the field in order that the "All Blacks" might chant their weird and inspiring war cry. The Wigan players first gave three hearty cheers, and then there was complete silence. "Bumper" Wright, as captain of the New Zealanders, came out of the ranks, surveyed his men, and then led them in the following war chant:—

Ka mate; ka mate; kaora, ka ora; ka mate; ka mate; ka ora, ka ora; Tenei te tanagata; puhuru huru; Nana o piiki inai; whaka white to ra; Hupanei Hupanei, Hupanei, Hupanei; whiti te ra.

Here is the translation:—"There is going to be a fight between us, may it mean death to you and life to us. We will fight on until one side is vanquished; so long as the daylight lasts we are here to continue the battle, to be either killed or victorious." It was very interesting to watch the players as they proclaimed their war notes, in a kind of action song.

Coming to something more prosaic the spin of the coin resulted in Leytham having the choice of ends, and he decided to play towards the mountainous district in the first half, and amidst intense excitement the teams went in position for the commencement of the struggle. "Bumper" Wright gave the initial "bump" to the leather, and J. Thomas responded on behalf of Wigan. From this kick Byrne marked, and landed the ball in the direction of Sharrock, who found himself in the grip of a stalwart New Zealander before he had time to think of getting the leather away.

CROWD BREAKS IN—LEYTHAM BREAKS THROUGH.

The crowd at the Greenough-street end pressed forward with such vigour in their excitement that the rails gave way. As the "All Blacks" were driven back to safer quarters the spectators were also induced to resume their original places. Wynyard, however, returned, and made a spirited attempt to force his way through, but he found that the tackling of the Wiganers was very effective. Tom Thomas was responsible for carrying the hostilities to half way, and he then handed the ball to Blears, who tried to furnish Leytham with an opening. The Wigan captain, however, is a little faster than the forward named, and he was a yard in front of Blears when he received the pass. Then Jenkins gave Leytham the ball after a fine dash, and it was evident that there was trouble in store for the "All Blacks." Messenger made a big effort to stop the Wigan captain, but he failed, and the Leicester exponent was then faced by Turtill, "the last of his race." With one of those pretty pieces of footwork which have made him famous, Leytham punted over the New Zealand full back's head, easily beat that player for speed, and grounded the leather near the corner. There was a perfect roar at this early and brilliant success, and as Leytham was registering the try the crowd near that corner also broke in. Hats were sent flying in the air, and there was great rejoicing. Leytham just failed to crown the effort by adding a goal, the ball travelling a trifle wide of the posts.

The *Wigan Examiner* reflected the excitement of the first Northern Union All Blacks tour with an in-depth full-page spread of the match.

scores in front at 9-3. From the restart, Jenkins dribbled the ball through the tourists' defence, picking up on the bounce as he 'managed to dodge past practically the whole New Zealand team'. It was Wigan's fourth and final try. This time it was Leytham's turn to miss the kick. It was a failure that looked costly ten nerve-wracking minutes from the end after Wigan's 12-3 lead was reduced to 12-8, the result of the visitors grabbing their second try through Adam Lile and Turtill converting. Wigan held on for victory, hat-trick hero Leytham deservedly being carried from the field.

The tourists' 'five-eighths' Lance Todd, who joined Wigan at the conclusion of the tour and was destined to become a Rugby League legend.

WIGAN v. NEW ZEALAND

Match statistics:
Wigan 12 New Zealand 8
Tour match
Saturday 9 November 1907 at Central Park, Wigan (kick-off: 3.00 p.m.)

Wigan	**New Zealand**
(cherry and white hoops)	(black)
Full-back:	
Jim Sharrock	Hubert Turtill (goal)
Three-quarters:	
Jimmy Leytham (captain, 3 tries)	Edgar Wrigley (try)
Bert Jenkins (try)	Harold Rowe
Tommy Thomas	Dally Messenger
Joe Miller	George Smith
Half-backs:	
Frank Battersby	Lance Todd
Johnny Thomas	Dick Wynard
Forwards:	
Jimmy Blears	Con Byrne
Bob Brooks	Tom Cross
Walter Cheetham	Adam Lile (try)
Dick Ramsdale	Charlie Pearce
Dick Silcock	Bill Tyler
William Wilcock	Hercules Wright (captain)
Trainer:	*Tour manager:*
Jack Hesketh	Harry Palmer
Referee: H. Farrar (Keighley)	*Half-time:* 6-3
Attendance: 30,000	*Receipts:* £1,249

First half:

3 min.	Leytham (Wigan)	try	3-0
15 min.	Wrigley (New Zealand)	try	3-3
— min.	Leytham (Wigan)	try	6-3

Second half:

62 min.	Leytham (Wigan)	try	9-3
65 min.	Jenkins (Wigan)	try	12-3
70 min.	Lile (New Zealand)	try	12-6
	Turtill (New Zealand)	conversion	12-8

WIGAN v. OLDHAM Lancashire Challenge Cup final
19 December 1908, Wheater's Field, Broughton

Wigan's 1908 Lancashire Cup success was the second by the club, having won the inaugural contest in 1905. Since transferring to Central Park in 1902, Wigan had built a formidable side, meeting Oldham, their biggest Lancastrian rivals at the time, five times in major finals from 1908 to 1913. Although a miserable, dark day following heavy morning rain, this first decider between the two fired the imagination, producing a record crowd and receipts for the final.

Wigan came close to a try in the opening minutes with Fred Gleave and Walter Cheetham each held short of the try-line. It was Oldham, though, that gained first points, Alf Wood kicking a penalty after Wigan was ruled offside. In difficult, muddy conditions, chances presented themselves at both ends before Oldham's Tom Llewellyn put George Cook in at the corner following a good attacking move from New Zealand centre George Smith, Wood missing the conversion. Wigan responded when Gleave, breaking down the left after a scrum, gave the ball to William 'Massa' Johnston (the big forward operating as an 'extra' three-quarter) who charged over. Wigan failed to level when Jimmy Leytham missed the easy kick, the first-half scoring concluding with each side adding a penalty through Wood and Jim Sharrock.

Following the interval, during which players had mud sponged from their faces and several were issued with clean jerseys, Wigan's pack began to get on top of the opposing set and Leytham came close to scoring his team's second try, being pulled back for a forward pass. With mist descending and visibility poor, Leytham levelled the scores at 7-7 after Wigan was awarded a penalty for a foul on Lance Todd but missed a further attempt shortly after. Oldham regained their lead when Wood kicked his third penalty, leading to a spell of pressure on the Wigan line. With the cup seemingly going to Oldham, Wigan – with the most exciting move of the match – scored the winning try eight minutes from the end. The Cherry and Whites won a scrum on their own 25 and Gleave, although struggling with a shoulder injury, broke away. The ball transferred via Johnny Thomas and Bert Jenkins to Todd, who

WIGAN TRIUMPH.

| TITANIC STRUGGLE AT BROUGHTON. | "GREEK MEETS GREEK." |

Oldham Vanquished after a Great Game.

CUP WON BY ONE POINT.

THE CONQUERING HEROES' RETURN.

Above: The *Wigan Examiner* headline writer decided to wax lyrical following the success over Oldham.

Right: Skipper Jimmy Leytham, whose second-half penalty goal pulled Wigan level.

raced down the touchline before kicking inside. Thomas got his foot to it, outpacing Wood in an exciting race to the line which put Wigan ahead for the first time. With visibility almost zero, Wigan fans shouted 'time' as they anxiously awaited the final whistle before claiming victory.

Match statistics:
Wigan 10 Oldham 9
Lancashire Challenge Cup final
Saturday 19 December 1908 at Wheater's Field, Broughton (kick-off: 2.40 p.m.)

Wigan	**Oldham**
(cherry and white hoops)	(white)
Full-back:	
Jim Sharrock (goal)	Alf Wood (3 goals)
Three-quarters:	
Jimmy Leytham (captain, goal)	George Tyson
Bert Jenkins	George Smith
Lance Todd	Tom Llewellyn
Joe Miller	George Cook (try)
Half-backs:	
Johnny Thomas (try)	Tom White
Fred Gleave	Billy Dixon
Forwards:	
Jack Barton	Bert Avery
Walter Cheetham	Joe Ferguson (captain)
Massa Johnston (try)	Billy Longworth
Dick Ramsdale	Bill Nansen
Dick Silcock	Arthur Smith
Tom Whittaker	Jim Wright
Trainer:	
Jack Hesketh	

Referee: Frank Renton (Hunslet) *Half-time:* 5-7
Attendance: 21,000 *Receipts:* £584
Weather: Rain, muddy conditions, very dark

First half:

12 min.	Wood (Oldham)	penalty	0-2
20 min.	Cook (Oldham)	try	0-5
28 min.	Johnston (Wigan)	try	3-5
30 min.	Wood (Oldham)	penalty	3-7
38 min.	Sharrock (Wigan)	penalty	5-7

Second half:

48 min.	Leytham (Wigan)	penalty	7-7
61 min.	Wood (Oldham)	penalty	7-9
72 min.	Thomas (Wigan)	try	10-9

WIGAN v. OLDHAM Northern Rugby League Championship final
1 May 1909, The Willows, Salford

Wigan claimed their first Championship success in the 1908/09 season, defeating Oldham in atrocious conditions at The Willows, Salford. It was a case of 'first-time lucky' for the Cherry and Whites, who tasted victory in their first appearance in the decider, whereas for Oldham it was their third consecutive defeat in the final. Wigan's hard-fought 7-3 win was also revenge for twelve months earlier when Oldham had won 12-5 in the semi-final stage at their Watersheddings home.

All the scoring came in the first half, with Wigan opening the account after three minutes with a penalty from skipper and flying winger 'Gentleman' Jimmy Leytham, following a foul on Lance Todd. Minutes later, Oldham, backed by the strong wind, grabbed the first try of the afternoon when forward Billy Jardine scored near the right corner flag following some scrambling play on the Wigan line to take the initiative at 3-2. The Central Park side were reduced to twelve men when full-back Jim Sharrock received a kick on the neck from Oldham's Arthur Smith as he tried to cover the ball during a 'rush' by the opposing forwards. Although Sharrock did not return until after the interval, the depleted Wigan side came up with what proved the winning score as Johnny Thomas and Leytham combined with forward Walter Cheetham to create an opening for Dick Ramsdale to cross under the posts. Leytham scored the final points of the day as he added the goal to put Wigan 7-3 ahead, an unexpected interval-lead considering Leytham had lost the toss, forcing Wigan to face the fierce wind during the first period.

Jim Sharrock (left), who was injured during the final, and Bert Jenkins.

The opening stages of the second half was the only time in the match when Oldham were on top as their pack started to dominate proceedings and, during an onslaught on the Wigan line, they came very close to scoring. Had they done so, they could well have taken the title, try opportunities being at a premium in deteriorating conditions. Wigan withstood the assault, and the closing 20 minutes were a virtual stalemate. While Oldham were considered to have better forwards, there was no doubt that Wigan had the superior backs. Leytham stood out in the three-quarter line, his partnership with centre Bert Jenkins being particularly eye-catching. The only blot on Wigan's historic day was the dismissal of Cheetham along with Oldham's Arthur Smith in the closing stages for fighting, both having played 'roughly' according to one scribe, who added: 'They might, with advantage to the game, have left the field earlier.'

Match statistics:
Wigan 7 Oldham 3
Northern Rugby League Championship final
Saturday 1 May 1909 at The Willows, Salford (kick-off: 3.00 p.m.)

Wigan	**Oldham**
(white)	(blue)
Full-back:	
Jim Sharrock	Alf Wood
Three-quarters:	
Jimmy Leytham (captain, 2 goals)	George Tyson
Bert Jenkins	Sid Deane
Lance Todd	Tom Llewellyn
Joe Miller	George Smith
Half-backs:	
Johnny Thomas	Billy Dixon
Neddy Jones	George Anlezark
Forwards:	
Jack Barton	Bert Avery
Walter Cheetham	Joe Ferguson (captain)
Howell de Francis	Billy Jardine (try)
Dick Ramsdale (try)	Joe Owens
Dick Silcock	Arthur Smith
Tom Whittaker	Harry Topham

Trainer:
Jack Hesketh

Referee: Jimmy Lumley (Leeds)   *Half-time:* 7-3
Attendance: 12,000   *Receipts:* £630
Weather: Heavy rain, gale-force wind, muddy conditions

First half:

3 min.	Leytham (Wigan)	penalty	2-0
15 min.	Jardine (Oldham)	try	2-3
30 min.	Ramsdale (Wigan)	try	5-3
	Leytham (Wigan)	conversion	7-3

Second half:
No scoring took place during the second half

WIGAN v. HUDDERSFIELD Northern Union Challenge Cup round three
29 March 1913, Central Park, Wigan

Central Park quickly became a 'Mecca' for rugby fans and large crowds were a common occurrence. The visit of Huddersfield's famed 'Team of All Talents' in the third round of the 1913 Challenge Cup created tremendous interest, with a new ground record attendance of 32,000 gaining admission, a figure claimed as the highest recorded for a Northern Union match at the time. It remained the largest Wigan crowd until 1920 when 33,843 turned up for a League match, again against Huddersfield. With tramcars, coaches and special trains pouring excited fans into Wigan, it was evident not everyone would gain entry. The gates closed ten minutes before the start, and an estimated two to three thousand, many from Huddersfield, were locked out.

When the game got underway it was Huddersfield who were on top in the early stages, coming close to crossing the Wigan line on several occasions. The home fans' hopes rose after their side finally made headway into Huddersfield territory, centre Frank Walford being stopped a yard short by Huddersfield skipper Harold Wagstaff. Soon afterwards, in the 17th minute, Johnny Thomas – Wigan's best performer on the day – received a pass from half-back partner Fred Gleave and elected to drop a goal, giving his side a 2-0 lead. Wigan applied further pressure, Thomas just failing to double the score when his penalty attempt hit the crossbar. The Fartowners regained the initiative and Wagstaff broke, sending James Davies in for the opening try, Wigan full-back Jim Sharrock being off the field for treatment. Major Holland missed the goal but Huddersfield led 3-2 at the break, although Davies reportedly dislocated his jaw in scoring.

The second half began disastrously for Wigan when Holland, following his own high kick, collared Sharrock as he attempted to clear, forcing him to spill it. From the resultant scrum, Huddersfield winger Albert Rosenfeld scored at the corner, Edgar Wrigley missing the goal. Wigan rallied, led by their forwards, and Thomas burst through a gap, passing to Walford, who put Bert Jenkins in for a try. Sharrock missed the conversion, but Wigan only trailed 6-5. The Cherry and Whites lost an opportunity to take control when Arthur Francis and Percy Coldrick split the visitors' defence, Percy Williams dropping the latter's pass with the line open. Instead, Huddersfield increased their lead, Duggie Clark forcing his way in at the corner and Tommy Gleeson diving over Sharrock. Holland added the touchline goal for the latter to end the scoring. Huddersfield had lived up to their title as 'the finest team in the Union', although Wigan missed influential forward Charlie Seeling, injured a week earlier.

KNOCKED OUT.

A RECORD ATTENDANCE

35,000 People at Central Park.

A record Central Park crowd (which was actually 32,000), but disappointment for the home fans.

Match statistics:
Wigan 5 Huddersfield 14
Northern Union Challenge Cup round three
Saturday 29 March 1913 at Central Park, Wigan (kick-off: 3.30 p.m.)

Wigan	*Huddersfield*
(cherry and white hoops)	(claret with narrow gold hoops)

Full-back:
Jim Sharrock (captain)	Major Holland (goal)

Three-quarters:
Robert Curwen	Albert Rosenfeld (try)
Bert Jenkins (try)	Edgar Wrigley
Frank Walford	Harold Wagstaff (captain)
Lance Todd	Tommy Gleeson (try)

Half-backs:
Fred Gleave	Tommy Grey
Johnny Thomas (drop goal)	James Davies (try)

Forwards:
Percy Coldrick	Duggie Clark (try)
Arthur Francis	John Chilcott
Bill Melling	Ben Gronow
Dick Ramsdale	John Higson
Dick Silcock	Aaron Lee
Percy Williams	Fred Longstaff

Trainer:
Jack Hesketh	A. Bennett

Referee: Arnett Smith (Halifax)   *Half-time:* 2-3
Attendance: 32,000   *Receipts:* £1,189
Weather: Dry, strong wind

First half:

17 min.	Thomas (Wigan)	drop goal	2-0
— min.	Davies (Huddersfield)	try	2-3

Second half:

45 min.	Rosenfeld (Huddersfield)	try	2-6
48 min.	Jenkins (Wigan)	try	5-6
56 min.	Clark (Huddersfield)	try	5-9
— min.	Gleeson (Huddersfield)	try	5-12
	Holland (Huddersfield)	conversion	5-14

WIGAN v. OLDHAM Northern Rugby League Championship final
6 May 1922, The Cliff, Broughton

The 1922 Championship final brought Wigan into opposition with old adversaries Oldham. It was claimed that more coaches left the borough for The Cliff ground than for any previous match. Wigan were missing star back Danny Hurcombe through injury, being replaced by Ted Smith who had helped the reserves win the final of the Lancashire Senior Competition the previous Wednesday.

The ever-reliable boot of Jim Sullivan opened the score, landing a penalty after Sid Jerram was obstructed. Centre Tommy Howley doubled the lead when he dropped a goal after Oldham full-back Ernie Knapman lost possession. The first real try-scoring chance favoured Oldham who, after Jerram dropped the ball, moved it quickly across to centre Billy Hall. He appeared to have the line at his mercy, but chose to feed wing-partner Jim Finnerty who failed to hold on. A few moments later, Oldham had a chance on the other flank through Reg Farrar but again the ball went to ground. The two sides continued to press and there were several close calls at each end, both teams tackling strongly. Sullivan scored the final points of the half with a magnificent goal from near the halfway line. It was taken from a 'mark' (a now defunct practice) made by Jerry Shea in fielding an Oldham dropout.

In the second half both teams continued to create chances, Sullivan almost scoring a try, just being beaten to the touchdown by Hall, after kicking beyond Knapman. The next score, the only one from Oldham, was also from a mark. Tom Woods' dropout for Wigan was fielded by Oldham's Maurice Tighe, who made the call, Farrar kicking an easy goal. With the score at 6-2, Oldham started to move the ball around, searching for the try that could put them ahead, but disaster struck. Alf Bates threw out a pass inside his own 25-yard area that was intercepted by Shea, who raced for the line. Heading for the corner, he sidestepped Knapman before cutting inside to go around Hall and behind the posts, evading Farrar's attempted tackle. Sullivan added the goal, putting Wigan 11-2 in front. It was the only try of the match and it settled the destination of the title. Two minutes from time, Jerram was brought down a yard short. Oldham forward Rod Marlor (who a few minutes

Above: Another triumph for Wigan over Oldham!

Right: An opportunity to relive the glory at a choice of Wigan theatres!

earlier had been involved in an altercation with Sullivan) kicked out at the half-back and was promptly dismissed, the resultant Sullivan penalty completing the scoring.

For Wigan – who had finished second to Oldham in the League table – it was their second championship.

Match statistics:
Wigan 13 Oldham 2
Northern Rugby League Championship final
Saturday 6 May 1922 at The Cliff, Broughton (kick-off: 3.30 p.m.)

Wigan	**Oldham**
(blue)	(red and white hoops)

Full-back:
Jim Sullivan (4 goals)	Ernie Knapman

Three-quarters:
Tom Coles	Jim Finnerty
Tommy Howley (goal)	Billy Hall
Jerry Shea (try)	Evan Davies
Ted Smith	Reg Farrar (goal)

Half-backs:
Sid Jerram	Alf Bates
George Hesketh	Maurice Tighe

Forwards:
Harry Banks	Fred Brown
Percy Coldrick (captain)	Jack Collins
Wilf Hodder	Herman Hilton (captain)
Fred Roffey	Rod Marlor
Ernie Shaw	Bob Sloman
Tom Woods	Alf Tomkins

Trainer:
Tommy McCarty	Charles Marsden

Referee: Bob Robinson (Bradford) *Half-time:* 6-0
Attendance: 26,000 *Receipts:* £1,825
Weather: Bright sunshine, strong wind

First half:
4 min.	Sullivan (Wigan)	penalty	2-0
7 min.	Howley (Wigan)	drop goal	4-0
33 min.	Sullivan (Wigan)	goal from mark	6-0

Second half:
45 min.	Farrar (Oldham)	goal from mark	6-2
63 min.	Shea (Wigan)	try	9-2
	Sullivan (Wigan)	conversion	11-2
78 min.	Sullivan (Wigan)	penalty	13-2

WIGAN v. OLDHAM Rugby League Challenge Cup final
12 April 1924, The Athletic Grounds, Rochdale

Pre-match forecasters reckoned Wigan would have to subdue the 'great Oldham forwards' if they were to secure their first Challenge Cup win. This they accomplished in style in the most memorable Challenge Cup final to date, scoring all five tries watched by a British record attendance of over 40,000. With many locked out, scenes inside were unprecedented, the crowd spilling onto the pitch and mounted police having to push them back.

After Jim Sullivan failed with an earlier attempt for Wigan, Ernie Knapman opened the scoring with a difficult penalty kick following a scrum infringement. Two minutes later Wigan's Fred Roffey got the first try, Fred Brown having dribbled the ball before picking up to provide the scoring pass. This encouraged the Cherry and Whites to open out play, the match having been dominated by the packs in a tentative opening.

After half an hour, Wigan scored a try that has entered Rugby League folklore. Tommy Parker, having received a pass from Jack Price, found himself hemmed in, but somehow managed to kick the ball as he turned. South African wing Attie van Heerden won the chase ahead of Joe Corsi, evading Knapman to cross the try-line at the corner. He then ran around the back of a mounted police horse situated inside the touch in-goal area before placing the ball behind the posts! Sullivan's

Oldham star duo Ernie Knapman (left), who opened the scoring, and Sid Rix.

The artist's headline for this cartoon strip takes a disparaging view of the Wigan opposition!

goal put Wigan six points up, the game stopping for a few minutes while officials and police tried to move the crowd back. Just before half-time, Albert Brough landed an Oldham goal after Wigan were penalised at a scrum.

With the crowd still close to the playing area, the referee, Reverend Frank Chambers, decided to turn around without the customary break. Another bizarre incident occurred when players collided with a man on crutches, breaking one of them! All the scoring in the second period went the way of Wigan. Parker registered a try in the corner 'practically among the spectators' after Danny Hurcombe had broken through and then Tommy Howley recovered a loose ball, transferring to Price, who 'disappeared from view' as he scored at the corner! Sullivan missed both kicks, making amends with a penalty just inside the Oldham half. It was all Wigan now and, having intercepted a pass by Corsi, Johnny Ring sprinted past Sid Rix and Knapman to score near the posts, with Sullivan converting. Oldham had their best chance to score a try soon after, Knapman just failing after chasing his own kick, but the day belonged to Wigan, their forwards having 'played the game of their lives.'

Harry Banks – a prominent member of a Wigan pack that was outstanding in the final.

Match statistics:
Wigan 21 Oldham 4
Rugby League Challenge Cup final
Saturday 12 April 1924 at The Athletic Grounds, Rochdale (kick-off: 3.30 p.m.)

Wigan	**Oldham**
(blue)	(white)

Full-back:
Jim Sullivan (3 goals)   Ernie Knapman (goal)

Three-quarters:
Johnny Ring (try)   Sid Rix
Tommy Howley   Billy Hall
Tommy Parker (try)   Alan Woodward
Attie van Heerden (try)   Joe Corsi

Half-backs:
Sid Jerram   George Hesketh
Danny Hurcombe   Alf Bates

Forwards:
Bert Webster   Jack Collins
Harry Banks   Ambrose Baker
George van Rooyen   Alf Tomkins
Fred Brown   Bob Sloman
Fred Roffey (try)   Albert Brough (goal)
Jack Price (captain, try)   Herman Hilton (captain)

Trainer:
Tommy McCarty   Charles Marsden

Referee: Reverend Frank Chambers (Dewsbury)   *Half-time:* 8-4
Attendance: 40,786   *Receipts:* £3,714
Weather: Cloudy, sunny spells, slight wind

First half:

15 min.	Knapman (Oldham)	penalty	0-2
17 min.	Roffey (Wigan)	try	3-2
30 min.	van Heerden (Wigan)	try	6-2
	Sullivan (Wigan)	conversion	8-2
38 min.	Brough (Oldham)	penalty	8-4

Second half:

47 min.	Parker (Wigan)	try	11-4
55 min.	Price (Wigan)	try	14-4
60 min.	Sullivan (Wigan)	penalty	16-4
70 min.	Ring (Wigan)	try	19-4
	Sullivan (Wigan)	conversion	21-4

Wigan v. Flimby and Fothergill United
Challenge Cup round one, 14 February 1925, Central Park, Wigan

Wigan's 116-0 Challenge Cup victory in 1925 against Cumbrian amateurs Flimby and Fothergill United has, over the years, become something of a Rugby League legend, rivalling Huddersfield's 119-2 win against Swinton Park (another junior outfit) in the 1914 competition. Predictably, considering it was played on 14 February, Wigan's huge win is remembered today as 'the St Valentine's Day Massacre' with the scoreline, Jim Sullivan's twenty-two goals and forty-four points, and Johnny Ring's seven tries all creating new club records which, with the exception of the latter, still stand today.

The amateurs came to Central Park unbeaten in that season's Cumberland League, having won 18 and drawn 2 of their 20 games, scoring an impressive 225 points to 25. There was certainly plenty of interest in the tie, with many Cumbrians travelling down to join the curious 12,000 crowd. They must have felt increasingly anxious as the match unfolded, one reporter stating their team 'were neither sturdy enough nor speedy enough to stem the avalanche of tries.'

Ring began his septet in the second minute after Flimby had enterprisingly breached the Wigan 25-yard area in the opening exchanges only to miscue a kick which was easily recovered by Sullivan. Instead of his usual kick downfield, Sullivan elected to run, passing to Ring, who then transferred the ball to centre Tommy Howley, accepting its return to score behind the posts. A few minutes later, Attie van Heerden on the other Wigan flank went over for the second try, crossing the Cumbrian try-line three more times in the next 16 minutes, although not increasing his tally further during the remaining hour of play. Other first-half tries went to Howley, George van Rooyen (the mighty South African forward 'scattering defenders in his wake'), David Booysen and Danny Hurcombe, with Ring adding two more.

If the beleaguered amateurs expected an easier ride in the second period, van Rooyen quickly dispelled the idea, making another powerful charge to score near the posts within a minute of the re-commencement. Loose-forward Jack Price got the next, three minutes later, going on to complete a second-half hat-trick. Further tries were claimed by Booysen, Hurcombe (both scoring two as each completed trebles) and Tom Beetham, while Ring grabbed another four on the way to his club record. The Flimby players felt the pace during the second half and even withdrawing behind their own try-line for Sullivan's conversion attempts was taking its toll! Winger Robley stood on the sidelines (hidden behind a sympathetic van Rooyen) for one of them, but was reprimanded by the referee when he tried it a second time!

SULLIVAN

Jim Sullivan – a club record 22 goals and 44 points!

Wigan v. Flimby and Fothergill United

Match statistics:
Wigan 116 Flimby and Fothergill United 0
Rugby League Challenge Cup round one
Saturday 14 February 1925 at Central Park, Wigan

Wigan	Flimby and Fothergill United
Full-back:	
Jim Sullivan (22 goals)	J. Ritson
Three-quarters:	
Johnny Ring (7 tries)	? Peel
Tommy Howley (try)	H. Atkinson (captain)
Danny Hurcombe (captain, 3 tries)	T. Ackerley
Attie van Heerden (4 tries)	J. Robley
Half-backs:	
George Owens	J. Ackerley
David Booysen (3 tries)	B. Atkinson
Forwards:	
Tom Beetham (try)	D. Holliday
Billy Banks	M. Richardson
Carl Burger	? Little
George van Rooyen (2 tries)	J. Lewis
Fred Roffey	? Davidson
Jack Price (3 tries)	? Irving
Trainer:	*Trainer:*
Tommy McCarty	J. Hodgson

Referee: R.H. Cooper (Hull)   *Half-time*: 53-0
Attendance: 12,000   *Receipts*: £520
Weather: Fine and dry

First half:

2 min.	Ring/Sullivan (Wigan)	try/conversion	5-0
4 min.	van Heerden/Sullivan (Wigan)	try/conversion	10-0
10 min.	van Heerden (Wigan)	try	13-0
12 min.	van Heerden/Sullivan (Wigan)	try/conversion	18-0
15 min.	Howley/Sullivan (Wigan)	try/conversion	23-0
18 min.	van Heerden/Sullivan (Wigan)	try/conversion	28-0
20 min.	Ring/Sullivan (Wigan)	try/conversion	33-0
22 min.	van Rooyen/Sullivan (Wigan)	try/conversion	38-0
24 min.	Booysen/Sullivan (Wigan)	try/conversion	43-0
30 min.	Hurcombe/Sullivan (Wigan)	try/conversion	48-0
36 min.	Ring/Sullivan (Wigan)	try/conversion	53-0

Second half:

42 min.	van Rooyen/Sullivan (Wigan)	try/conversion	58-0
45 min.	Price/Sullivan (Wigan)	try/conversion	63-0
48 min.	Ring/Sullivan (Wigan)	try/conversion	68-0
52 min.	Booysen/Sullivan (Wigan)	try/conversion	73-0
54 min.	Hurcombe/Sullivan (Wigan)	try/conversion	78-0
56 min.	Booysen/Sullivan (Wigan)	try/conversion	83-0
59 min.	Ring/Sullivan (Wigan)	try/conversion	88-0
62 min.	Ring (Wigan)	try	91-0
65 min.	Hurcombe/Sullivan (Wigan)	try/conversion	96-0
67 min	Price/Sullivan (Wigan)	try/conversion	101-0
70 min.	Price/Sullivan (Wigan)	try/conversion	106-0
75 min.	Beetham/Sullivan (Wigan)	try/conversion	111-0
77 min.	Ring/Sullivan (Wigan)	try/conversion	116-0

WIGAN v. WARRINGTON Northern Rugby League Championship final
8 May 1926, Knowsley Road, St Helens

Wigan secured their third Championship in the midst of Britain's first general strike, invoked by the Trades Union Congress in support of the striking miners. The all-out stoppage was into its sixth day (it lasted ten), and disrupted public transport, but many Wigan supporters managed to secure conveyance to St Helens, while others walked to the ground! Their reward was to see their heroes defeat second-placed Warrington 22-10, the first time since 1915 the League-leaders had taken the title.

Warrington centre Ned Catterall converted a penalty to put his side in front when South African half David Booysen passed the ball after being grounded. Johnny Ring had the chance to put Wigan ahead moments later, dropping the ball with the line open. He soon made amends when, ball in hand, he raced to the opposite flank, passing to Attie van Heerden, who put the supporting Tommy Howley in for the first try. Jim Sullivan missed the kick, while, at the other end, Catterall did likewise with a penalty that would have put the Wires back in front. Warrington were under pressure, and midway through the half Howley was the creator of a second Wigan try, neatly sidestepping several defenders to send Ring flying over in the corner. Five minutes later, Booysen broke down the middle, transferring to Tommy Parker, who sent van Heerden on a clear run over the line, Sullivan's goal making it 11-2. There was no further score before the break, although van Heerden almost got his second touchdown, his attempt to ground the ball being thwarted after kicking towards the Warrington try-line.

Warrington opened the second half in determined mood as George Walker, Tommy Flynn, Fred Ryder and Jimmy Tranter stood out during a sustained spell of pressure. Yet their luck was out when Howley intercepted, regaining his short grubber kick past full-back Arthur Frowen to score what looked a killer try. To their credit, Warrington hit back and a forward 'rush' was capitalised on by Ryder, who put Alf Peacock over. Catterall's goal reduced the margin to 14-7. Wigan had a battle on as the opposition pack raised the stakes, Tommy Roberts and Walker both being

Wigan's 1925/26 team (including four players in 'civvies') before a match at Dewsbury in October 1925. From left to right, back row: Jack Price, Wilf Hodder, Bob Ilsley, Frank Stephens, George van Rooyen, John Sherrington, Tom Beetham, Fred Roffey, Sid Jerram. Front row: Jim Sullivan, George Owens, David Booysen, Danny Hurcombe, Sol Oakley, Johnny Ring, Tommy Howley, Attie van Heerden.

held short of the try-line. Again they had the misfortune to be intercepted, Parker gratefully accepting the ball, quick passing via Howley sending Ring sprinting over. Sullivan's goal made it 19-7. Wigan were back in full flow, Ring completing his hat-trick eight minutes from time with a try in the corner. The Wires captain Ryder completed the scoring, going over after a Sullivan clearance was charged down.

Match statistics:
Wigan 22 Warrington 10
Northern Rugby League Championship final
Saturday 8 May 1926 at Knowsley Road, St Helens

Wigan	**Warrington**
(cherry and white hoops)	(primrose and blue)

Full-back:
Jim Sullivan (captain, 2 goals)	Arthur Frowen

Three-quarters:
Johnny Ring (3 tries)	Dick Blackburn
Tommy Howley (2 tries)	George Walker
Tommy Parker	Ned Catterall (2 goals)
Attie van Heerden (try)	Tommy Roberts

Half-backs:
George Owens	Tommy Flynn
David Booysen	Fred Ryder (captain, try)

Forwards:
Wilf Hodder	Billy Cunliffe
Jack Bennett	Alf Peacock (try)
Tom Beetham	Billy Harrop
George van Rooyen	Tom Cunliffe
Frank Stephens	Jimmy Tranter
Jack Price	Frank Williams

Trainer:
Tommy McCarty

Referee: Bob Robinson (Bradford)   *Half-time:* 11-2
Attendance: 20,000   *Receipts:* £1,100
Weather: Cloudy, windy

First half:

Time	Player	Type	Score
6 min.	Catterall (Warrington)	penalty	0-2
10 min.	Howley (Wigan)	try	3-2
20 min.	Ring (Wigan)	try	6-2
25 min.	van Heerden (Wigan)	try	9-2
	Sullivan (Wigan)	conversion	11-2

Second half:

Time	Player	Type	Score
52 min.	Howley (Wigan)	try	14-2
54 min.	Peacock (Warrington)	try	14-5
	Catterall (Warrington)	conversion	14-7
66 min.	Ring (Wigan)	try	17-7
	Sullivan (Wigan)	conversion	19-7
72 min.	Ring (Wigan)	try	22-7
79 min.	Ryder (Warrington)	try	22-10

WIGAN v. DEWSBURY Rugby League Challenge Cup final
4 May 1929, Wembley Stadium, London

One of the most historic days in Rugby League history came about on 4 May 1929, when Wigan met Dewsbury at what was then known as the Empire Stadium. It was reported the Wembley groundsmen spent all week removing the markings from the previous weekend's FA Cup final, the rugby posts being erected on Tuesday. Led by the renowned Jim Sullivan, the presence of Wigan in London could not have provided the sport with a better ambassador as it sought to raise the profile of the game. The Cherry and Whites also had the phenomenal pace and talent of Welsh wing ace Johnny Ring, whose 62 tries in 1925/26 is still a club record. While Wigan's classy backs made them pre-final favourites, Dewsbury captain Joe Lyman had faith in his team's forward power, saying: 'It was teamwork which pulled us through and I am putting my faith [in] teamwork at Wembley. Our forwards are as mighty a lot as I have known and I think they will upset the Wigan backs.'

The match was attended by numerous VIPs and politicians and the Australian Rugby League authorities sent a cablegram offering 'greetings and best wishes for the success of your venture at Wembley.' The game was broadcast live on BBC radio, with former referee Revd Frank Chambers providing the commentary.

In a day of many firsts, it was Wigan who had the distinction of kicking off the inaugural final, followed after just three minutes by scoring the first points from Sullivan's trusty boot, and then after 14 minutes by the opening try by Syd Abram. Sullivan's goal (a penalty) was taken in front of the posts from 30 yards out following an offside decision against Dewsbury hooker Percy Brown. Abram's effort, which came after Lyman had failed to level the scores with a penalty, was set up by his

Jim Sullivan leads out his side before the first ever Wembley showpiece.

Winning smiles! From left to right, standing: Lou Brown, Wilf Hodder, Frank Stephens, Jim Sullivan (with cup), John Sherrington, Jack Bennett, Len Mason, Tom Parker. Kneeling: Syd Abram, Johnny Ring, Arthur Binks.

scrum-half partner Arthur Binks. Binks, who had gathered a clearance kick from Harry Bland, sent Abram on a dash towards the flank, where he attempted to link up with New Zealand winger Lou Brown. With Brown covered, Abram continued his exciting run, outpacing full-back Jack Davies to touch down in the corner just as he was being tackled. Sullivan failed to convert but Wigan had a nerve-settling 5-0 advantage. It was full-back Davies who eventually gave Dewsbury's reportedly 3,000-strong following at the match something to cheer about, scoring his side's only points with an impressive drop goal from inside his own half. This encouraged the Yorkshire team, who pressed with more determination but were resisted, there being no further score before the half-time whistle.

Dewsbury continued in the same vein at the start of the second half and mounted a strong assault on the Wigan line, the Lancastrian's loose-forward John Sherrington bringing Lyman down from behind after he had broken clear, following a move that had covered half the field. After that scare, Wigan started to dominate, their forwards getting on top of the strong Dewsbury pack. On the hour their Scottish centre Roy Kinnear – father of the comedy actor of the same name – evaded Clifford Smith and Tommy Bailey and, when tackled by Davies, managed to shrug himself sufficiently free to hand the ball to Brown, who dived over in the corner. Sullivan again failed with the kick, hitting the crossbar, and moments later he hit the outside of a post with a penalty attempt. However, at 8-2, Wigan were now looking comfortable, being two scores ahead. With 15 minutes left to play, Dewsbury suffered a critical blow when their centre Herbert Hirst had to retire from the match

The Wigan team as it appeared in the 1929 Wembley programme.

with a fractured rib. With the influential Lyman relocating from loose-forward to replace him in the backs, it gave the Wigan halves more freedom and it was Binks, with ten minutes left, who created the final score. Sending a short kick past the Dewsbury line of defence, he scooted around Henry Coates and John Woolmore to retrieve the ball and put Kinnear in for a simple try beneath the posts. Sullivan's goal made the final score 13-2.

After receiving the famous trophy, jubilant captain Sullivan said: 'Our boys played really well but Dewsbury gave us a hard time', adding, 'Our players had the advantage of being used to playing before a large crowd.'

Match statistics:
Wigan 13 Dewsbury 2
Rugby League Challenge Cup final
Saturday 4 May 1929 at Wembley Stadium, London (kick-off: 3.00 p.m.)

Wigan	**Dewsbury**
(cherry and white hoops)	(red, amber and black hoops)

Full-back:

Jim Sullivan (captain, 2 goals)	Jack Davies (drop goal)

Three-quarters:

Johnny Ring	Tommy Bailey
Tom Parker	Clifford Smith
Roy Kinnear (try)	Herbert Hirst
Lou Brown (try)	Henry Coates

Half-backs:

Syd Abram (try)	John Woolmore
Arthur Binks	Jim Rudd

Forwards:

Wilf Hodder	James Hobson
Jack Bennett	Percy Brown
Tom Beetham	William Rhodes
Frank Stephens	Harry Bland
Len Mason	Joe Malkin
John Sherrington	Joe Lyman (captain)

Trainer:

Tommy McCarty	W.J. Hobbs

Referee: Bob Robinson (Bradford)   *Half-time:* 5-2
Attendance: 41,500   *Receipts:* £5,614
Weather: Cloudy, strong breeze

First half:

3 min.	Sullivan (Wigan)	penalty	2-0
14 min.	Abram (Wigan)	try	5-0
33 min.	Davies (Dewsbury)	drop goal	5-2

Second half:

60 min.	Brown (Wigan)	try	8-2
70 min.	Kinnear (Wigan)	try	11-2
	Sullivan (Wigan)	conversion	13-2

WIGAN v. SALFORD Northern Rugby League Championship final
28 April 1934, Wilderspool, Warrington

Wigan won their fourth Championship title in 1934, confounding pre-match expectations by beating Salford 15-3. Although current champions Salford were favoured by many, the Central Park faithful could point to a 'double' over their opponents during the season and, having looked championship 'no-hopers' months earlier, were enjoying an excellent run, winning eleven of their final twelve League matches to finish second.

Wigan lost the coin toss and subsequently found themselves facing a strong wind during the first half. It clearly did not deter the Cherry and Whites, although the first scoring opportunities – two failed penalty attempts from Gus Risman – went the way of Salford. It was Wigan centre Gwynne Davies who drew first blood in the tenth minute, intercepting a Salford pass after they had won a scrum in Wigan territory. Racing forward, he drew the Reds' full-back Harold Osbaldestin before transferring inside to the supporting Ossie Griffiths. Griffiths then went on a long run downfield, the ball returning through George Bennett into the hands of Davies, who scored near the posts, Sullivan adding the goal. Risman missed with two more penalty kicks, the second after a touch judge had raised his flag to signal a goal but was overruled by referee Dobson. Another Wigan try came just before the break, again resulting from a Salford error, Jack Morley recovering the ball on the halfway

Wigan 1933/34 with the Championship trophy. From left to right, back row: Charlie Seeling Jnr, Harold Edwards, Albert Davis, Bill Targett, Joe Golby, Reg Hathway, Ossie Griffiths. Middle row: Jack Morley, Len Mason, Jim Sullivan (captain), Dicky Twose, Joe Wilson, Gwynne Davies. Front: George Bennett, Hector Gee.

line after the Reds had lost possession. He evaded Bob Brown, delivering a perfect kick ahead that rested over the try-line. Morley then won the chase for the touchdown. With Sullivan again converting, Wigan held a 10-0 interval lead.

Predictably, Salford showed greater resolve in the second period and looked more threatening than in the opening 40 minutes. Their reward came when, from a scrum near the Wigan line, scrum-half Billy Watkins sped away to send Emlyn Jenkins in with a neat reverse pass, Risman again missing the goal. Wigan managed to regain the initiative and Bennett in particular came near to obtaining a third try for Wigan. Then Sullivan, following two abortive attempts from colleagues, landed a drop goal to edge his side 12-3 ahead. Wigan prop Bill Targett claimed the final points, his late try following good work by Davies and Bennett (again after Salford had spilled the ball) ensuring the League crown returned to Central Park. Sullivan's goal miss was academic, the final score being a comfortable 15-3.

The 31,564 crowd, which overflowed onto the pitch during the first half having taken up positions behind the posts and along the touchlines, produced record receipts for the final and the Warrington ground.

Match statistics:
Wigan 15 Salford 3
Northern Rugby League Championship final
Saturday 28 April 1934 at Wilderspool, Warrington (kick-off: 3.30 p.m.)

Wigan	*Salford*
(cherry and white hoops)	(red)

Full-back:
Jim Sullivan (captain, 3 goals)   Harold Osbaldestin

Three-quarters:
Jack Morley (try), Len Mason,   Les Pearson, Sammy Miller,
Gwynne Davies (try), Dicky Twose   Gus Risman, Bob Brown

Half-backs:
George Bennett, Hector Gee   Emlyn Jenkins (try), Billy Watkins

Forwards:
Bill Targett (try), Joe Golby,   Billy Williams (captain),
Harold Edwards, Reg Hathway,   Bert Day, Joe Bradbury,
Albert Davis, Ossie Griffiths   Aubrey Casewell,
          Alf Middleton, Jack Feetham

Player/coach: *Team manager:*
Jim Sullivan   Lance Todd

Referee: Albert Dobson (Featherstone)   *Half-time:* 10-0
Attendance: 31,564   *Receipts:* £2,114
Weather: Strong wind, soft ground conditions

First half:

10 min.	Davies (Wigan)	try	3-0
	Sullivan (Wigan)	conversion	5-0
38 min.	Morley (Wigan)	try	8-0
	Sullivan (Wigan)	conversion	10-0

Second half:

47 min.	Jenkins (Salford)	try	10-3
72 min.	Sullivan (Wigan)	drop goal	12-3
80 min.	Targett (Wigan)	try	15-3

WIGAN v. WAKEFIELD TRINITY Rugby League Challenge Cup final
4 May 1946, Wembley Stadium, London

For Wigan, making their second Wembley trip, having four players heading Down Under on the aircraft carrier HMS *Indomitable* with the Great Britain tour party was to prove a crucial factor. The four – Joe Egan, Ken Gee, Martin Ryan and Ted Ward – were all key members of the side, but the absence of goal-kicker Ward proved decisive as Wigan lost by just one point in a final hailed as a Wembley classic.

Wakefield, whose outstanding forward Harry Murphy was also on tour, should have opened the scoring, but centre and captain Billy Stott missed an early penalty. Instead, Wigan troubled the scoreboard first, with Jack Blan scoring a try following a dribbling rush at the line by the pack. Winger Brian Nordgren got a second, racing half the length of the field after a perfect Gordon Ratcliffe pass and placing the ball in the corner. Nordgren missed both conversions, but Wigan looked good value for their 6-0 lead with a quarter of the match played. After a nervous opening, Trinity rallied, veteran Stott proving a steadying influence. He almost scored after intercepting a pass and narrowly failed with a long-distance penalty attempt. Then he put winger Ron Rylance clear, Rylance returning the ball inside to Stott, who brushed aside two challengers before diving over Jack Cunliffe to score. Stott missed the conversion but made amends with a penalty five minutes before half-time, leaving the match finely balanced at 6-5 to Wigan.

On the resumption, Wakefield was first out of the blocks, with player-coach Jim Croston almost scoring. Continuing to press, Stott, of all people, dropped the ball. Stan Jolley picked up to race 70 yards to touch down in the corner. Nordgren again

George Banks completes a tackle watched by Jack Blan (9) as Wakefield attempt to clear their line at Wembley.

missed the kick, leaving Wigan 9-5 up. Stott made amends for his misdemeanour seven minutes later, crossing the try-line unopposed but failing to add the crucial extra points. Trinity now trailed by one point. The pendulum swung back to Wigan, Cunliffe making a telling break to put Nordgren in. The New Zealander again missed the conversion, and their 12-8 lead left Wakefield still within striking distance. It looked ominous when Croston forced his way over, but Stott again missed the goal, leaving the Cherry and Whites hanging on 12-11 in front. With just over a minute left, Wigan were penalised for obstruction inside their own 25, ten yards from the touchline, with Stott kicking the winning goal on the way to becoming the first recipient of the Lance Todd Trophy, named after the former Wigan player, for his Man of the Match performance.

Match statistics:
Wigan 12 Wakefield Trinity 13
Rugby League Challenge Cup final
Saturday 4 May 1946 at Wembley Stadium, London (kick-off: 3.30 p.m.)

Wigan	**Wakefield Trinity**
(cherry and white hoops)	(blue with red band)

Full-back:
Jack Cunliffe — Billy Teall

Three-quarters:
Brian Nordgren (2 tries), Gordon Ratcliffe — Ron Rylance, Billy Stott (captain,
Ernie Ashcroft, Stan Jolley — 2 tries 2 goals), Jim Croston (try),
Denis Baddeley (try)

Half-backs:
Reg Lowrey — Johnny Jones
Tommy Bradshaw — Herbert Goodfellow

Forwards:
George Banks, Jack Blan (try) — Harry Wilkinson, Len Marson,
Frank Barton, Harry Atkinson, — Jim Higgins, Mick Exley,
Eddie Watkins (captain), Billy Blan — Derek Howes, Len Bratley

Coach:
Jim Sullivan

Player/team manager:
Jim Croston

Referee: Alf Hill (Leeds)
Attendance: 54,730
Weather: Sunny and hot

Half-time: 6-5
Receipts: £12,013

First half:

7 min.	J. Blan (Wigan)	try	3-0
19 min.	Nordgren (Wigan)	try	6-0
25 min.	Stott (Wakefield)	try	6-3
35 min.	Stott (Wakefield)	penalty	6-5

Second half:

50 min.	Jolley (Wigan)	try	9-5
57 min.	Stott (Wakefield)	try	9-8
65 min.	Nordgren (Wigan)	try	12-8
71 min.	Croston (Wakefield)	try	12-11
79 min.	Stott (Wakefield)	penalty	12-13

Wigan overcame their Wembley disappointment of fourteen days earlier to win the Championship final in style at Manchester City's Maine Road ground, watched by a massive 67,000 attendance, 10,000 of which were estimated to have travelled from Wigan. The Cherry and Whites – who actually played in blue for this match – took to the field using the same thirteen players that had lined up under the Twin Towers against Wakefield Trinity.

In the early exchanges, Wigan appeared to struggle, and came close to conceding the first try when Jeff Bawden crossed the line but was prevented from touching down by Jack Cunliffe. Shortly after, Bawden landed a penalty when Gordon Ratcliffe was judged offside. Brian Nordgren must have thought his Wembley goal-kicking nightmare was about to repeat itself when he attempted a penalty shortly after, his boot hitting the turf and the ball travelling a short distance along the ground. He was probably a relieved man when his second effort, from a difficult position, put the teams level. Wigan started to open out and were rewarded when Ernie Ashcroft, backing up a fine break by young prop Frank Barton, scored near the posts. Nordgren's – and Wigan's – frustration continued when he missed the simple kick. Although Wigan were getting on top, Huddersfield still had plenty to offer, with Les Baxter and John Anderson both coming close to scoring a try and Bob Robson failing with a drop goal attempt. Yet Wigan went into the break with a narrow 5-2 lead.

Coach Jim Sullivan changed his formation at half-time; Reg Lowrey going on the left wing, Stan Jolley moving inside to left centre and Ashcroft relocating to stand-off. The changes had a positive effect on their attacking play and, although Bawden closed Huddersfield's deficit to one point through a penalty seven minutes

VICTORY IN FINAL

Wigan Win League Championship Cup

After having been beaten in the Lancashire Cup final and the Rugby League Challenge Cup final, Wigan added the Rugby League Championship Cup to the Lancashire League Cup by a glorious victory over Huddersfield in the final on Saturday, on the Manchester City association ground at Maine Road. Huddersfield, playing against the wind in the first half, many times seemed to have the Wigan defence in a tangle with some swift passing, but just when success looked likely something happened to save the Wigan line—either weak finishing or an unexpected tackle when all seemed lost.

Although Wigan held a lead of three points at the interval, their prospects looked none too rosy, especially when injuries occurred; but, infusing all their energy into the game, they wore down their opponents and won by a convincing margin. It was the sixth time the club have won the Rugby League Championship, including one war-time success.

Interest in the match was very great. Followers of the club began the trip to Manchester very early in the morning and, in addition to the large number who travelled by the normal trains, thousands took advantage of the six extra trains, and it is computed that fully 10,000 Wiganers attended the match.

As the colours of the two competing clubs clashed somewhat, one side had to change. Wigan lost the toss on this point, so they had to play in blue. Consequently the sellers of rosettes provided themselves with both cherry and white—the Wigan colours for over half-a-century—and blue. The majority of people preferred to wear cherry and white.

The Wigan players and directors travelled by motor coach and when they reached Maine Road the large crowd could be seen on the top of the high embankment in the ground. It had been expected that the attendance would create a record for a Rugby League game in this country—over 69,504 on the occasion of the League final between Salford and Castleford, on the same ground, in 1939—

PRESENTATION OF THE CUP

The Cup was presented to Eddie Watkins, the Wigan captain, by Mr. A. A. Bonner, chairman of the Rugby League Management Committee, who congratulated Wigan on their success.

THE TEAM'S RETURN

The Wigan team and directors left Manchester by motor coach and from Hindley to Wigan the Cup was held aloft by Eddie Watkins. There were groups of enthusiasts on the pavements all the way and cheers were given for the players. At the top of King-street and Wallgate a large number of people had waited for some time in order to give the victorious team a great welcome. Another crowd assembled outside Central Park, and after the players had entered the pavilion there were shouts for the team to bring the Cup out again. This was done.

After refreshments had been served to the assembly, Mr. H. L. Platt, chairman of directors, said he was sure no one would contend that the success that day was not a just reward; they had concluded one of the greatest seasons in the history of the club. The winning of the Rugby League Championship Cup had been due to fine team spirit, and the second half was a grand example of a team playing with great enthusiasm.

Wigan captured the first post-war Championship with 'a glorious victory'.

into the half, they started to dominate play. It was while Cunliffe had moved temporarily to stand-off while recovering from a bout of concussion that he scored the second try, receiving a quick pass from scrum-half Tommy Bradshaw following a scrum. Nordgren missed with the goal attempt, leaving Wigan 8-4 ahead. The final try was claimed by Ashcroft, who, having received a pass from Bradshaw 25 yards from the Huddersfield line, cut inside before neatly sidestepping full-back Bill Leake. Nordgren added the goal from in front of the posts to extend the final margin to 13-4.

For Eddie Watkins, who broke his thumb during the game, it was a special moment, receiving the trophy as Wigan captain in the absence of Great Britain tourist and regular skipper Joe Egan.

Match statistics:
Wigan 13 Huddersfield 4
Northern Rugby League Championship final
Saturday 18 May 1946 at Maine Road, Manchester (kick-off: 3.30 p.m.)

Wigan	**Huddersfield**
(blue)	(claret and gold)

Full-back:	
Jack Cunliffe (try)	Bill Leake

Three-quarters:	
Brian Nordgren (2 goals)	John Anderson
Gordon Ratcliffe	Alex Fiddes (captain)
Ernie Ashcroft (2 tries)	Bill Davies
Stan Jolley	Jeff Bawden (2 goals)

Half-backs:	
Reg Lowrey	Tommy Grahame
Tommy Bradshaw	Glyn Morgan

Forwards:	
George Banks	Ken Mallington
Jack Blan	Harold Whitehead
Frank Barton	Joe Bradbury
Eddie Watkins (captain)	Jack Aspinall
Harry Atkinson	Les Baxter
Billy Blan	Bob Robson

Coach:
Jim Sullivan

Referee: Albert Dobson (Featherstone)   *Half-time:* 5-2
Attendance: 67,136   *Receipts:* £8,386
Weather: Cloudy, windy, some sunshine

First half:

10 min.	Bawden (Huddersfield)	penalty	0-2
26 min.	Nordgren (Wigan)	penalty	2-2
36 min.	Ashcroft (Wigan)	try	5-2

Second half:

47 min.	Bawden (Huddersfield)	penalty	5-4
55 min.	Cunliffe (Wigan)	try	8-4
66 min.	Ashcroft (Wigan)	try	11-4
	Nordgren (Wigan)	conversion	13-4

WIGAN v. DEWSBURY Northern Rugby League Championship final
21 June 1947, Maine Road, Manchester

Wigan retained their grip on the Championship in 1947 in a match that pre-empted the arrival of summer Rugby League forty-nine years later, the final taking place on the third Saturday in June after a severe winter had extended the season. Interestingly, the attendance of 40,599 – almost 27,000 down on last year's final at the same Maine Road venue – was considered a good turnout for that time of year! The Cherry and Whites repeated their previous scoreline in defeating Dewsbury 13-4, although the match did not achieve the same heights. It was, nonetheless, another record-breaking day for the Central Park outfit, their sixth title being the most achieved by any club up to that time. Wigan began as favourites, having topped the table for the second successive year.

Dewsbury's outstanding full-back Jimmy Ledgard gave his side an early lead with a drop goal after fielding a Wigan dropout. This was after Ledgard himself had created pressure in the opening minutes through an excellent kick to the corner flag, the resulting play forcing Jack Cunliffe to kick the ball dead. Ted Ward missed two penalty opportunities to draw level – a long-range effort dipping under the crossbar and another difficult kick hitting the post. Wigan almost got over the try-line when Johnny Lawrenson stepped into touch as he raced to the corner after one slick attack but, as the first half wore on, Dewsbury began to outplay their more illustrious opponents, holding on to their slender 2-0 lead until half-time.

The second session was a different affair, as Wigan rediscovered their form to score a Brian Nordgren try two minutes after the break. The opening was created by a clever kick from Ken Gee, which was recovered by Ward, who sped down the

Dewsbury's Jimmy Ledgard (nearest camera) watches as the penalty attempt from Wigan's Ted Ward (third player from left in distance) sails wide of the left-hand upright.

right flank before sending the New Zealand wing in at the corner. Ward added the difficult kick, the ball going in off the far post to give Wigan a three-point advantage. This was a rallying call for the Cherry and Whites, and they began to dominate, aided by the temporary absence of Dewsbury's injured Arthur Street. Lawrenson and Ernie Ashcroft each went close to scoring before the two combined to send the former over near the corner flag. Ward missed the kick but the tide was now flowing in Wigan's favour. Three minutes later, Wigan scored their third try when Tommy Bradshaw, from a scrum, exchanged passes with Lawrenson on the blind side to score, with Ward augmenting. Dewsbury fought desperately to get back, but their only reward was a late Jack Holt drop goal.

Match statistics:
Wigan 13 Dewsbury 4
Northern Rugby League Championship final
Saturday 21 June 1947 at Maine Road, Manchester (kick-off: 3.00 p.m.)

Wigan	**Dewsbury**
(cherry and white hoops)	(red, amber and black hoops)

Full-back:
Jack Cunliffe — Jimmy Ledgard (goal)

Three-quarters:

Brian Nordgren (try)	Des Armitage
Ted Ward (2 goals)	Geoff Clark
Ernie Ashcroft	Kenneth Sacker
Johnny Lawrenson (try)	George Withington

Half-backs:

Cec Mountford	Cyril Gilbertson
Tommy Bradshaw (try)	Harry Royal (captain)

Forwards:

Ken Gee	Harry Hammond
Joe Egan (captain)	Vince McKeating
George Banks	Ben Pearson
Frank Barton	Frank Cox
Billy Blan	Jack Holt (goal)
Jack Blan	Arthur Street

Coach:	*Coach:*
Jim Sullivan	Vic Hey

Referee: Albert Dobson (Pontefract)
Attendance: 40,599
Weather: Cloudy, some sunshine

Half-time: 0-2
Receipts: £5,894

First half:

3 min.	Ledgard (Dewsbury)	drop goal	0-2

Second half:

42 min.	Nordgren (Wigan)	try	3-2
	Ward (Wigan)	conversion	5-2
59 min.	Lawrenson (Wigan)	try	8-2
62 min.	Bradshaw (Wigan)	try	11-2
	Ward (Wigan)	conversion	13-2
76 min.	Holt (Dewsbury)	drop goal	13-4

Wigan v. New Zealand tour match
22 October 1947, Central Park, Wigan

Wigan's third meeting with a New Zealand touring side (the others being 1907 and 1926) produced a match considered the best at Central Park for many years and described in one newspaper as 'an epic of the handling code, packed with thrills and brilliant football'. It was a match that put stand-off Cec Mountford – signed by Wigan the previous year – into opposition with brother Ken, who was the visitors scrum-half. With a touch of theatre, the two sides walked out side by side before the tourists performed their usual war dance.

Cec Mountford was instrumental in Gordon Ratcliffe's opening try, which was scored at the corner following a bright start by Wigan, although Ted Ward failed with the kick. The home fans were then entertained with some sizzling rugby from the Kiwis. Persistence paid off for the tourists and, launching an attack down the right flank, they levelled the scores when winger Jack Forrest cut inside to place the ball near the posts. Full-back Warwick Clarke added the goal to put his team two points ahead. Wigan fought hard to hit back, with Ernie Ashcroft coming close, but the New Zealanders retained their lead until the half-time break.

After the interval, Ken Mountford increased the tourists' advantage by scoring a great try after Clarke, Doug Anderson and Charlie McBride had combined to create the opening, Clarke's second conversion making it 10-3. At this point, Wigan's play became more urgent and they began throwing everything at their opponents, with Cec Mountford in particular having an inspired game against his fellow-countrymen. Gordon Ratcliffe, Brian Nordgren and Joe Egan were each stopped just short of the try-line before Billy Blan finally got over, running on to a high pass from Egan to score near the posts. With Ward kicking the goal, it closed the gap to 10-8 in the New Zealanders' favour. Wigan now sensed victory could be theirs and

The Wigan team before the match against New Zealand. From left to right, back row: Jack Bowen, Billy Blan, Gordon Ratcliffe, Frank Barton, Ted Ward, Brian Nordgren, Ernie Ashcroft. Front row: Martin Ryan, Joe Egan (captain), Tommy Bradshaw, Ken Gee, Cec Mountford, George Banks.

attacked relentlessly, aided by the fact that they had dominated the scrums throughout the match. The visitors, however, who were pinned inside their own 25-yard area, impressed with the quality of their defence. Ward (who had moved up to support the Wigan three-quarter line) and Ratcliffe were both pushed into touch near the corner flag, the former also just failing with a penalty goal attempt. One scribe said: 'It seemed impossible for New Zealand to continue to hold out against repeatedly strong and well-planned attacks but the great-hearted tackling succeeded.' And hold out they did to achieve a win in a match 'which will be remembered as long as New Zealand teams come to this country.'

Match statistics:
Wigan 8 New Zealand 10
Tour match
Wednesday 22 October 1947 at Central Park, Wigan (kick-off: 4.15 p.m.)

Wigan	**New Zealand**
(cherry and white hoops)	(black with double white V)

Full-back:
Martin Ryan   Warwick Clarke (2 goals)

Three-quarters:

Brian Nordgren	Jack Forrest (try)
Ted Ward (goal)	Morrie Robertson
Ernie Ashcroft	Doug Anderson
Gordon Ratcliffe (try)	Arthur McInnarney

Half-backs:

Cec Mountford	Roy Clark
Tommy Bradshaw	Ken Mountford (try)

Forwards:

Ken Gee	Les Pye
Joe Egan (captain)	Pat Smith (captain)
George Banks	Joffe Johnson
Frank Barton	Charlie McBride
Billy Blan (try)	Jack Newton
Jack Bowen	Travers Hardwick

Coach: *Coach:*
Jim Sullivan   Thomas McClymont

Referee: W. Stockley (Leigh)   *Half-time:* 3-5
Attendance: 24,089   *Receipts:* £2,588
Weather: Overcast

First half:

5 min.	Ratcliffe (Wigan)	try	3-0
23 min.	Forrest (New Zealand)	try	3-3
	W. Clarke (New Zealand)	conversion	3-5

Second half:

51 min.	Mountford (New Zealand)	try	3-8
	W. Clarke (New Zealand)	conversion	3-10
60 min.	Blan (Wigan)	try	6-10
	Ward (Wigan)	conversion	8-10

WIGAN v. BRADFORD NORTHERN Rugby League Challenge Cup final
1 May 1948, Wembley Stadium, London

Wigan were back at Wembley for a third time, facing holders Bradford Northern with the chilling knowledge that their Yorkshire rivals had won 15-3 at Central Park just seven days earlier in a Championship play-off semi-final. The rematch certainly caught the supporters' imagination, Wigan being followed by a reported 15,000 to London, and Bradford having 10,000 voices behind them. This all contributed to the first 90,000-plus Challenge Cup final turn-out. It was also the first final attended by a reigning monarch, King George VI, who met the two teams before the match and presented the trophy to a proud Joe Egan afterwards. The only thing to spoil an otherwise perfect occasion was the untypical Wembley weather of heavy rain and a driving wind, making playing conditions difficult.

In a low-scoring final, Wigan had the first try-scoring opportunity when Tommy Bradshaw, Cec Mountford and Ted Ward linked up to send winger Gordon Ratcliffe on a 50-yard run. Kicking ahead, Ratcliffe looked certain to score under the posts, but he turned awkwardly and the chance was lost. Wigan did eventually make the first strike when Bradford wing Eric Batten, having mishandled the ball, attempted to kick downfield only for Jack Hilton to charge it down and dribble past Batten to

The teams enter the vast Wembley arena led by their respective captains; Ernie Ward of Bradford Northern (left) and Wigan's Joe Egan.

dive over in the corner for a try. Ted Ward, having failed with two earlier penalties, kicked the goal from near the touchline, placing Wigan 5-0 up with a quarter of the match gone. Northern responded quickly, Alan Edwards pouncing on a kick into the left corner from loose-forward Ken Traill, Ratcliffe trying in vain to fall on it first. Ernie Ward made a poor attempt at the conversion. Batten almost made amends for his earlier error but lost the ball in the greasy conditions with the try-line open, Northern returning to the sanctuary of the dressing room trailing by two points.

The second half was almost a stalemate with Wigan generally on top but Bradford, inspired by Lance Todd winner Frank Whitcombe, defending stoutly. Wigan's Bill Hudson and Bradford's Trevor Foster came closest to recording tries, but the only score of the half came in the final minutes. It occurred when Bradford had to drop out from under their posts. Wigan's second-row pair Les White and Billy Blan dribbled the ball back over the try-line, prop Frank Barton dropping on it for a try. Ted Ward surprisingly hit the post with the simple kick due to the slippery conditions, but Wigan were assured of victory 8-3. An unsung hero was Hudson, who 'policed' Traill, Bradford's biggest threat the previous week.

Match statistics:

Wigan 8 Bradford Northern 3
Rugby League Challenge Cup final
Saturday 1 May 1948 at Wembley Stadium, London (kick-off: 3.00 p.m.)

Wigan	**Bradford Northern**
(cherry and white hoops)	(white with red, amber and black V)

Full-back:
Martin Ryan   Billy Leake

Three-quarters:
Gordon Ratcliffe, Ted Ward (goal)   Eric Batten, Des Case
Ernie Ashcroft   Ernie Ward (captain)
Jack Hilton (try)   Alan Edwards (try)

Half-backs:
Cec Mountford, Tommy Bradshaw   Willie Davies, Donald Ward

Forwards:
Ken Gee, Joe Egan (captain),   Frank Whitcombe, Vic Darlison,
Frank Barton (try), Les White,   Herbert Smith, Barry Tyler,
Billy Blan, Bill Hudson   Trevor Foster, Ken Traill

Coach: *Team manager:*
Jim Sullivan   Dai Rees

Referee: George Phillips (Widnes)   *Half-time:* 5-3
Attendance: 91,465   *Receipts:* £21,121
Weather: Heavy rain, strong wind

First half:

20 min.	Hilton (Wigan)	try	3-0
	Ward (Wigan)	conversion	5-0
24 min.	Edwards (Bradford)	try	5-3

Second half:

79 min.	Barton (Wigan)	try	8-3

WIGAN v. AUSTRALIA tour match
20 October 1948, Central Park, Wigan

The visit of the 1948 Kangaroos to take on the might of Ken Gee, Joe Egan and company was eagerly anticipated by Central Park devotees, who paid £3,300, record receipts for a Wigan match against a touring side. The 28,554 attendance was only surpassed by the three Test matches during the Australians' twenty-seven-match tour.

The home team quickly stamped their authority on the game with two tries in the opening ten minutes from wingmen Johnny Lawrenson and Gordon Ratcliffe. Lawrenson struck after seven minutes, beating Pat McMahon and Clive Churchill on a touchline run for an excellent try in the left corner. Three minutes later, Cec Mountford was the creative force, finding a gap for Ted Ward to put Ratcliffe in at the opposite corner. Ward missed the target with both touchline conversion efforts. A third try almost came Wigan's way when Ernie Ashcroft intercepted an Australian pass to go charging through, only for wing partner Lawrenson to be covered when a score looked certain. At this point, it was all Wigan, whose skill with the ball was thrilling their supporters. Then, against the run of play, the tourists found an opening for Johnny Graves to go flying over the Wigan line for a touchdown, leaving Ratcliffe and Martin Ryan trailing in his wake. With the momentum turning towards the visitors, Alf Gibbs snatched the ball from a Wigan player during a tackle to race over, despite the attention of Mountford. Graves added the two points, having failed to convert his own try, and this left Wigan trailing, rather unexpectedly, by 8-6 at half-time.

Jim Sullivan's interval dressing room talk obviously motivated Wigan, who came out with renewed vigour. Ratcliffe had almost put Nat Silcock over before Ashcroft got himself on the scoresheet, accepting the final pass of an across-the-field move to score near the posts. Ward registered his first goal and Wigan led 11-8. It was all

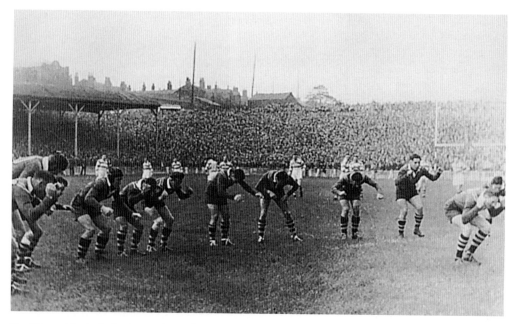

The Wigan side, in the background, watch as their Australian guests perform their 'war-dance'.

Wigan again and the crowd was brought to its toes when Ratcliffe covered 70 yards to finish off a move begun on the Wigan 25-yard line by scrum-half Johnny Alty. Ward's goal put supporters in a confident mood at 16-8 with just over 20 minutes remaining. Winger Pat McMahon closed the scoring with an Australian consolation try, Graves hitting the woodwork with his kick. With the gap at five points, play became 'heated' in the final minutes, the Australians accused of some over-exuberant tactics. When the final whistle sounded, Wigan fans celebrated a famous victory over a team that included eight Test players.

Match statistics:
Wigan 16 Australia 11
Tour match
Wednesday 20 October 1948 at Central Park, Wigan (kick-off: 4.30 p.m.)

Wigan	*Australia*
(cherry and white hoops)	(green with double gold V)

Full-back:
Martin Ryan — Clive Churchill

Three-quarters:

Gordon Ratcliffe (2 tries)	Pat McMahon (try)
Ted Ward (2 goals)	Johnny Graves (try, goal)
Ernie Ashcroft (try)	Bobby Dimond
Johnny Lawrenson (try)	Len Pegg

Half-backs:

Cec Mountford	Wally O'Connell
Johnny Alty	Bill Thompson

Forwards:

Ken Gee	Bill Tyquin (captain)
Joe Egan (captain)	Duncan Hall
Frank Barton	Jack Rayner
Nat Silcock	Nevyl Hand
Harry Atkinson	Alf Gibbs
Billy Blan	Kevin Schubert (try)

Coach:	*Tour managers:*
Jim Sullivan	W. Buckley and E. Simmonds

Referee: Charlie Appleton (Warrington)
Attendance: 28,554
Weather: Overcast, damp conditions

Half-time: 6-8
Receipts: £3,317

First half:

7 min.	Lawrenson (Wigan)	try	3-0
10 min.	Ratcliffe (Wigan)	try	6-0
15 min.	Graves (Australia)	try	6-3
27 min.	Schubert (Australia)	try	6-6
	Graves (Australia)	conversion	6-8

Second half:

46 min.	Ashcroft (Wigan)	try	9-8
	Ward (Wigan)	conversion	11-8
59 min.	Ratcliffe (Wigan)	try	14-8
	Ward (Wigan)	conversion	16-8
62 min.	McMahon (Australia)	try	16-11

WIGAN v. HUDDERSFIELD Northern Rugby League Championship final
13 May 1950, Maine Road, Manchester

The headline in the *Wigan Examiner* proclaimed this match 'The finest Wigan victory of all time' and few could dispute the magnitude of their success, achieved without eight of their finest players, all of them with the Great Britain tour party in Australia. The eight – Ernie Ashcroft, Tommy Bradshaw, Jack Cunliffe, Joe Egan, Ken Gee, Jack Hilton, Gordon Ratcliffe and Martin Ryan – sent their colleagues a telegram offering their 'best wishes for Saturday' and asking for the result to be cabled to them immediately after the match. One can only imagine their amazement when that 20-2 score travelled down the wire later. Conversely, Huddersfield, whose wonderfully talented side of that era was aided by Colonial power, particularly among the backs, had no one involved in the tour. It was noted by the press that on a very hot day in energy-sapping conditions, Wigan started the game looking the stronger and more energetic and finished in the same manner, a testimony to the training regime of Jim Sullivan.

It was high-speed winger Brian Nordgren that gave Huddersfield an early sample of what to expect when he beat three defenders on a brilliant touchline run before being tackled. It was only a temporary reprieve, however, as fellow New Zealander Cec Mountford scythed his way through Huddersfield centres Jeff Bawden and Pat Devery in a quicksilver move to link up with makeshift winger Nat Silcock. Silcock – normally a second-row forward who had spent most of the season in the reserves – crashed over after only three minutes play. Ted Ward added the difficult kick. The Fartowners strove desperately to get back into the

The programme cover featuring the two Commonwealth captains: Australian Pat Devery (Huddersfield, left) and New Zealander Cec Mountford (Wigan).

Stand-in Wigan winger Nat Silcock scores the opening try after just three minutes.

match, trying to set up their star Australian wing Lionel Cooper – scorer of 60 tries the previous season – but it was to no avail and the Yorkshire side were clearly shaken by the early try, making several handling errors. Wigan maintained the pressure and loose-forward Billy Blan was almost over for a second touchdown, being pushed into touch near the corner flag. It was clearly not Huddersfield's day when, while passing the ball inside their own half, Nordgren cut inside to intercept and score near the corner, another excellent Ward goal making it 10-0. Wigan came close to registering further tries through Nordgren and Blan, before Huddersfield at last showed what they were capable of and started to look threatening. Dick Cracknell and Cooper each tested the Wigan line a couple of times, with Wigan centre George Roughley standing out in defence when twice bringing off excellent tackles. As the first half closed, Bawden attempted to open Huddersfield's account with a long-range penalty, but it sailed wide.

Bawden scored with his next attempt, however, just two minutes into the second period following an obstruction. Despite that encouragement, it was Wigan that looked the stronger of the two, one report saying Huddersfield 'showed signs of tiring whereas Wigan were full of energy.' The Fartowners were dominating scrum possession – as they had in the opening half – but found their most effective method of advancing downfield into Wigan territory was to kick. The potential threat posed by Cooper was kept under wraps thanks to an impressive defensive display by Silcock and, eventually, Wigan broke loose again, scrum-half Johnny Alty racing through a gap and heading rightwards to feed Jack Broome. Broome outpaced the defence before 'dummying' to wing-partner Silcock, turning inside for a terrific try behind the posts. Ward's goal made it 15-2, virtually assuring Wigan of a major upset with only 12 minutes' play remaining on the clock. Several more let-offs followed for Huddersfield before prop Ted Slevin created space for Blan – who lost five front teeth during the match – to score near the

WIGAN v. HUDDERSFIELD

The vast Maine Road crowd in the background looks on as Huddersfield wing Dick Cracknell (with ball) attempts to escape his pursuing opposite number, Brian Nordgren (nearest camera, on left).

Wigan's magnificent thirteen with the Championship trophy. From left to right: Johnny Alty, Harold McIntyre, George Roughley, Ted Slevin, Bill Hudson, Frank Barton, Jack Broome, Jack Large, Brian Nordgren, Ted Ward, Nat Silcock, Billy Blan, Cec Mountford (captain).

corner, Ward again augmenting through another wonderful touchline effort. When the final whistle sounded a few minutes later, the 20-2 victory meant Wigan had won the championship a record seventh time, once more than Huddersfield.

It was a case of déjà vu for Huddersfield, having lost at the same stage to Wigan four years earlier when the Central Park team had four players absent on the previous British tour to the Antipodes. Triumphant coach Jim Sullivan said after the match: 'There was never any doubt from the first that we would win. We achieved success against what seemed impossible odds, all by first-class teamwork and superior fitness and finish. I am very proud of them. What would we have felt like if Huddersfield, with eight of their best players away, had beaten us with a full team as we beat them today?'

Most felt that Huddersfield, in facing an 'unknown quantity' with Wigan's much-changed line-up, lost their composure when Wigan raced into a surprise ten-point lead in the early stages. Only Nordgren and Mountford (an excellent team leader in the absence of skipper Egan) among the backs and Slevin, Frank Barton, Bill Hudson and Blan in the pack had appeared regularly throughout the season with the first team. Among the rest, Broome, Harold McIntyre and Jack Large featured in around half the fixtures. Silcock was singled-out by the press for praise because of the way the fourteen-stone forward had contained the threat of speed-merchant Cooper on the wing.

The 65,000 attendance produced takings of £11,500, a record for a match played outside of Wembley.

Match statistics:
Wigan 20 Huddersfield 2
Northern Rugby League Championship final
Saturday 13 May 1950 at Maine Road, Manchester (kick-off: 3.00 p.m.)

Wigan	*Huddersfield*
(cherry and white hoops)	(white with claret and gold band)

Full-back:
Ted Ward (4 goals)	Johnny Hunter

Three-quarters:
Nat Silcock (try)	Dick Cracknell
Jack Broome (try)	Jeff Bawden (goal)
George Roughley	Pat Devery (captain)
Brian Nordgren (try)	Lionel Cooper

Half-backs:
Cec Mountford (captain)	Russ Pepperell
Johnny Alty	Billy Banks

Forwards:
Ted Slevin	John Daly
Harold McIntyre	James Mundy
Frank Barton	Arthur Wilmot
Bill Hudson	Ken Morrison
Jack Large	Bob Nicholson
Billy Blan (try)	Ike Owens

Coach:
Jim Sullivan

Referee: Matt Coates (Pudsey)   *Half-time:* 10-0
Attendance: 65,065   *Receipts:* £11,500
Weather: Sunny and hot

First half:
3 min.	Silcock (Wigan)	try	3-0
	Ward (Wigan)	conversion	5-0
15 min.	Nordgren (Wigan)	try	8-0
	Ward (Wigan)	conversion	10-0

Second half:
42 min.	Bawden (Huddersfield)	penalty	10-2
68 min.	Broome (Wigan)	try	13-2
	Ward (Wigan)	conversion	15-2
75 min.	Blan (Wigan)	try	18-2
	Ward (Wigan)	conversion	20-2

WIGAN v. WARRINGTON Lancashire Challenge Cup final
4 November 1950, Station Road, Swinton

Wigan continued their post-Second World War domination of the sport with this emphatic victory over Warrington at Station Road, Swinton, watched by a record Lancashire Cup attendance of 42,541 (only the 42,793 at the 1953 Wigan–St Helens final would subsequently be higher), paying record receipts for the competition of £6,222.

Nat Silcock, restored to the second row after deputising on the wing in the absence of the 1950 tourists, gave Warrington an early warning of what was to come by outwitting three opponents before he was hauled down close to the line. Ken Gee and Jack Broome also went near before the ball was whipped out to the left, where full-back Jack Cunliffe raced up from the back as the 'extra man', taking his pass at speed to score the first try of the afternoon, Gee adding the goal. Warrington loose-forward Harold Palin reduced the margin five minutes later when Wigan skipper Cec Mountford strayed offside. The Cherry and Whites were playing at their brilliant best, backing up superbly and tackling well as a unit. Any threat from Warrington's legendary Australian wing Brian Bevan – scorer of 68 tries that season – was nullified through a fine afternoon's 'marking' by Brian Nordgren. It was inevitable that Wigan would add further tries before the break, and two were eventually scored through Nordgren and Ted Slevin. Nordgren's was executed without a hand being put upon him, having completed a move at speed when taking an inside pass from George Roughley. It was Nordgren who provided the final pass for Slevin's effort, Gee having made the initial break. Gee tagged on both goals, leaving the Wigan fans feeling very relaxed about their side's 15-2 interval lead.

Wigan went on to add three further tries in the second half through Roughley (scoring in the corner off a Nordgren pass), Nordgren (under the posts after a reverse pass from Roughley) and Johnny Alty (sprinting over from a play-the-ball ten yards out). Gee converted the last two, as Wigan built a commanding 28-2 lead. The Wires, who were handicapped for much of the second period by the loss of star half-back Gerry Helme with a cracked rib 27 minutes from time, finally got a try late on when centre Albert Naughton touched down in the corner. Minutes earlier Bevan had made a sizzling break, only to lose the ball as he dived under the posts.

It was a record-making fifth successive win for Wigan, a sequence that was extended to six the following season and a competition record that was never surpassed.

WARRINGTON WERE STAGGERED BY WIGAN'S SUPERB DISPLAY
Overwhelming Superiority in 5th Consecutive Lancashire Cup Victory

Wigan's '5th Consecutive Lancashire Cup Victory' came in a record-making sequence of six wins in the competition.

Match statistics:
Wigan 28 Warrington 5
Lancashire Challenge Cup final
Saturday 4 November 1950 at Station Road, Swinton (kick-off: 2.45 p.m.)

Wigan	**Warrington**
(cherry and white hoops)	(primrose and blue hoops)

Full-back:
Jack Cunliffe (try)   Eric Frodsham

Three-quarters:
Gordon Ratcliffe   Brian Bevan
Jack Broome   Ron Ryder
George Roughley (try)   Albert Naughton (try)
Brian Nordgren (2 tries)   Albert Johnson

Half-backs:
Cec Mountford (captain)   Bryn Knowelden
Johnny Alty (try)   Gerry Helme

Forwards:
Ken Gee (5 goals)   Billy Derbyshire
Ronnie Mather   Ike Fishwick
Frank Barton   Jim Featherstone
Ted Slevin (try)   Harry Bath (captain)
Nat Silcock   Bob Ryan
Billy Blan   Harold Palin (goal)

Coach: *Team manager:*
Jim Sullivan   Chris Brockbank

Referee: George Phillips (Widnes)   *Half-time:* 15-2
Attendance: 42,541   *Receipts:* £6,222
Weather: Cloudy, dry conditions

First half:

9 min.	Cunliffe (Wigan)	try	3-0
	Gee (Wigan)	conversion	5-0
14 min.	Palin (Warrington)	penalty	5-2
20 min.	Nordgren (Wigan)	try	8-2
	Gee (Wigan)	conversion	10-2
29 min.	Slevin (Wigan)	try	13-2
	Gee (Wigan)	conversion	15-2

Second half:

47 min.	Roughley (Wigan)	try	18-2
59 min.	Nordgren (Wigan)	try	21-2
	Gee (Wigan)	conversion	23-2
70 min.	Alty (Wigan)	try	26-2
	Gee (Wigan)	conversion	28-2
78 min.	Naughton (Warrington)	try	28-5

WIGAN v. BRADFORD NORTHERN Northern Rugby League
Championship final, 10 May 1952, Leeds Road, Huddersfield

Huddersfield Town AFC's Leeds Road ground provided the backdrop for the last major honour achieved by Wigan's magnificent side of the early post-Second World War era. The occasion was the Championship final, the opposition being League-leaders Bradford Northern.

As anticipated, it was the Bradford pack, particularly Barry Tyler and Ken Traill, that provided the biggest concern. Their backs, depleted by a shoulder injury to absent captain and centre Ernie Ward, never got into the match, with Len Haley's lack of pace at stand-off being cited as the root cause. Although they did not seriously threaten Wigan's line, Northern did lead twice, both times after a Joe Phillips penalty had provided the opening score for each half. Unlike Northern, Wigan's back division looked dangerous from kick-off, with full-back Martin Ryan continually linking up to provide extra width. After early pressure, Brian Nordgren crossed the whitewash but was judged to have stepped into touch and, when Wigan got caught offside at a play-the-ball, it was the Phillips boot that opened the scoring. It was a short-lived lead, Nat Silcock placing the ball near the posts five minutes later after Traill was penalised for not allowing Nordgren to play the ball, a quick tap catching Bradford off-guard for the score. Ken Gee added the goal before a second Phillips penalty (Johnny Alty transgressed at a scrum) reduced the half-time margin to one point.

Bradford appeared to benefit from the break, their pack winning more ball and looking stronger after the restart. Phillips' third penalty restored the Yorkshire team's lead at 6-5, although, as in the first period, it was not protected for long. Gee had

Wigan with their 1951/52 trophy haul. From left to right, standing: Maurice Hughes (coach), Harry Street, Billy Blan, Ernie Ashcroft, George Woosey, Ronnie Mather, Ronnie Hurst, Frank Barton, Bert Barnes (kit-man). Seated: Brian Nordgren, Martin Ryan, Ken Gee, Jack Cunliffe (captain), George Roughley, Jack Hilton, Gordon Ratcliffe. On ground: Johnny Alty, Len Constance. Trophies: Lancashire Cup, Championship, Lancashire League. The photograph was taken after Hughes had replaced Jim Sullivan as coach.

the first chance to regain the Wigan initiative, missing a penalty, and then Alty got Wigan motoring again with an exciting break, following which both Nordgren and Jack Large (the afternoon's outstanding performer) were held on the line. It was Gee, atoning for his earlier failure, who put Wigan ahead again with a penalty. It was a lead they did not surrender, registering two late tries through Jack Cunliffe and Ryan to assure victory. Cunliffe's effort came with 12 minutes left, making a great solo break before scoring in the left corner, Ryan's try being set up in almost the last move of the match through a slick pass from Alty.

The attendance of 48,684 was considered disappointing, most believing that the setting of a 55,000 limit had deterred many from travelling, particularly as the second half was broadcast on the radio. The victory concluded seven magnificent seasons in which the club won 16 major trophies overall.

Match statistics:
Wigan 13 Bradford Northern 6
Northern Rugby League Championship final
Saturday 10 May 1952 at Leeds Road, Huddersfield (kick-off: 3.00 p.m.)

Wigan	*Bradford Northern*
(cherry and white hoops)	(white with red, amber and black band)

Full-back:
Martin Ryan (try)   Joe Phillips (3 goals)

Three-quarters:
Jack Hilton, Jack Broome,   Bob Hawes, Joe Mageen,
George Roughley, Brian Nordgren   Norman Hastings, Jack McLean

Half-backs:
Jack Cunliffe (captain, try)   Len Haley
Johnny Alty   Gwylfa Jones

Forwards:
Ken Gee (2 goals), Ronnie Mather,   Bill Shreeve, Norman Haley,
George Woosey, Nat Silcock (try),   Brian Radford, Barry Tyler,
Jack Large, Harry Street   Trevor Foster (captain),
                          Ken Traill

Coach: *Coach:*
Jim Sullivan   Dai Rees

Referee: Charlie Appleton (Warrington)   *Half-time:* 5-4
Attendance: 48,684   *Receipts:* £8,215
Weather: Cloudy, strong wind

First half:
20 min.	Phillips (Bradford Northern)	penalty	0-2
25 min.	Silcock (Wigan)	try	3-2
	Gee (Wigan)	conversion	5-2
34 min.	Phillips (Bradford Northern)	penalty	5-4

Second half:
52 min.	Phillips (Bradford Northern)	penalty	5-6
62 min.	Gee (Wigan)	penalty	7-6
68 min.	Cunliffe (Wigan)	try	10-6
80 min.	Ryan (Wigan)	try	13-6

WIGAN v. WORKINGTON TOWN Rugby League Challenge Cup final
10 May 1958, Wembley Stadium, London

Wembley 1958 signalled a glorious comeback for Wigan following the break up of the magnificent side of the early post-war years. The new Wigan had in its ranks Eric Ashton, Billy Boston and Brian McTigue, three players who would represent the club a record-breaking six times at the famous venue in nine seasons. Wigan were the pre-final favourites, but Workington Town were no slouches, making their third trip to the Twin Towers since 1952, their confidence boosted through a Championship semi-final win at St Helens the previous weekend. The attendance of just over 66,000 was the lowest at the stadium since 1946 and some 12,000 down on the 1957 figure, the poor turnout being blamed on the BBC's first live coverage of the match since 1952. Wigan were forced to make a late change when regular loose-forward Roy Evans withdrew with a heavy cold. He was replaced by Bernard McGurrin. Only Jack Cunliffe (twice) had appeared at the stadium before, compared to five members of the Cumbrian side. Wing sensation Boston was in the unaccustomed role of centre, covering for veteran Ernie Ashcroft, who had broken a rib one month earlier.

It was an exciting final, with the result in doubt for almost the full 80 minutes. Wigan looked threatening as soon as the match kicked off, skipper Ashton almost breaking through in virtually the first move of the game and Boston then going on one of his typical blockbusting runs before Workington full-back John McAvoy managed to halt him with a try beckoning. David Bolton then broke away, but the chance was lost when he kicked high with Ashton and Terry O'Grady in support. Workington made Wigan rue those missed chances after 11 minutes, taking the lead when outstanding winger Ike Southward outpaced Mick Sullivan in a 35-yard dash to the try-line following a break by Brian Edgar, who parted with the ball as Cunliffe tackled him. Southward converted, and a few minutes later he almost scored again but failed to hold on to an interception. Wigan returned to the attack, and when O'Grady received the ball on the right flank, he cut inside to feed Boston, who sent Sullivan racing over in the corner. A magnificent Cunliffe goal levelled the

Mick Sullivan races over in the corner for Wigan's first try after receiving the ball from the grounded Billy Boston (4).

Midfield action as the Workington defence stifles a Wigan move.

scores at 5-5. At this stage Wigan were well on top and busy Welsh scrum-half Rees Thomas had a further try disallowed due to a forward pass. Workington were relying on their robust pack but Wigan were denying them possession by dominating the scrums. The second Wigan try came when O'Grady and Cunliffe created an opening for Thomas, who jinked past three defenders to feed prop John Barton, who crashed through two would-be tacklers to score. Cunliffe added the goal and the Central Park team were leading for the first time, 10-5. Southward pulled two points back before the interval, with a penalty after McTigue was judged to have obstructed.

Workington came out in the second half looking eager to regain their lead, but suffered a setback when their two twenty-one-year-old forwards Edgar and Andy Key had to leave the field for treatment. Wigan regained the initiative ten minutes into the half, McTigue finding himself in possession on the right side of the field near the try-line before dummying and sidestepping his way through to dive over in the corner. Cunliffe missed the kick, but Wigan were now leading by six points. Southward, having failed with a penalty attempt, succeeded with another effort after Wigan were penalised for a 'loose arm' in the scrum, bringing Town to within one score. The Cumbrians found a second wind, and McAvoy and Harry Archer both made tremendous breaks but lacked support each time. When Workington were awarded another penalty they took the bold decision of running with the ball

WIGAN v. WORKINGTON TOWN

Norman Cherrington. His last-ditch tackle frustrated Ike Southward's late bid to win the Cup for the Cumbrians.

instead, resulting in Archer and John O'Neil sending Southward on an exciting run down the touchline. Norman Cherrington made a desperate dive and the winger lost the ball with the impact, the match being won and lost at that moment.

The two sides had produced an exciting match for the television cameras, the Lance Todd award going to Thomas who said 'I never expected the Lance Todd Trophy, an appearance at Wembley and a medal all in one day. It has really shaken me!'

Match statistics:
Wigan 13 Workington Town 9
Rugby League Challenge Cup final
Saturday 10 May 1958 at Wembley Stadium, London (kick-off: 3.00 p.m.)

Wigan	**Workington Town**
(cherry and white hoops)	(white with blue band)

Full-back:
Jack Cunliffe (2 goals)   John McAvoy

Three-quarters:
Terry O'Grady   Ike Southward (try, 3 goals)
Eric Ashton (captain)   John O'Neil
Billy Boston   Danny Leatherbarrow
Mick Sullivan (try)   Bill Wookey

Half-backs:
David Bolton   Harry Archer
Rees Thomas   John Roper (captain)

Forwards:
John Barton (try)   Norman Herbert
Bill Sayer   Bert Eden
Brian McTigue (try)   Andy Key
Norman Cherrington   Brian Edgar
Frank Collier   Cec Thompson
Bernard McGurrin   Benny Eve

Coach: *Team manager:*
Joe Egan   Jim Brough

Referee: Ron Gelder (Wakefield)   *Half-time:* 10-7
Attendance: 66,109   *Receipts:* £33,175
Weather: Sunny, strong breeze

First half:

11 min.	Southward (Workington)	try	0-3
	Southward (Workington)	conversion	0-5
17 min.	Sullivan (Wigan)	try	3-5
	Cunliffe (Wigan)	conversion	5-5
28 min.	Barton (Wigan)	try	8-5
	Cunliffe (Wigan)	conversion	10-5
35 min.	Southward (Workington)	penalty	10-7

Second half:

50 min.	McTigue (Wigan)	try	13-7
61 min.	Southward (Workington)	penalty	13-9

WIGAN v. ST HELENS Northern Rugby League Championship
27 March 1959, Central Park, Wigan

This traditional Good Friday fixture entered the record books for attracting Rugby League's highest attendance (47, 747) for a League fixture and the biggest Central Park crowd in history. The previous Central Park record was 44,731 for the Barrow–St Helens Challenge Cup semi-final in April 1956, while the Wigan team's best had been 44,674 for the 1952 Good Friday clash with the Saints. Wigan and St Helens were the leading lights in the 1958/59 Championship race and produced a thriller. It was a match-up of two sides full of star names, including four of the greatest wingers in Rugby League history. Both were missing influential prop forwards; Wigan being without John Barton and St Helens missing Abe Terry. The crucial loss for Saints, however, was through their decision to drop centre and ace marksman Peter Fearis.

Alex Murphy, switched from his usual scrum-half position to stand-off, made the first clear break and raced towards the right corner but, when tackled by Fred Griffiths, his intended pass for Tom van Vollenhoven went astray. Derek Brown, designated as St Helens goal kicker for Fearis, missed a chance to open the scoring, his penalty attempt being blown back by the strong wind. It was Griffiths who got the first points, landing a 45-yard penalty after 'loose arm' in the scrum by Brian Briggs. A Wigan pass was intercepted by van Vollenhoven, their defence recovering when a try looked certain. Then Griffiths added a second penalty, a touchline effort after Dick Huddart was judged to have committed a foul while making a tackle. Things were not going St Helens way, and this was typified by the unusual sight of their fearsome loose-forward Vince Karalius missing a tackle on opposite number Roy Evans, enabling the Wigan man to race from 20 yards out to touch down, Griffiths adding the goal. Saints showed signs of rallying, and Jan Prinsloo almost scored but half-time was reached with Wigan holding a 9-0 advantage.

Two of Rugby League's all-time great wingers were in opposition; Wigan's Billy Boston (left) and St Helens' Tom van Vollenhoven.

After the restart, Wigan increased their lead when Keith Holden and Eric Ashton combined brilliantly to put Billy Boston through with a clear run under the posts, Griffiths converting. At 14-0 Wigan looked secure until, in a 15-minute burst, the Saints dramatically came back with four tries from Murphy, Wilf Smith, Doug Greenall (later discovered to have broken his arm) and Prinsloo. Brown, however, only converted the second effort. Sandwiched in between, Ashton scored what was effectively the winning try after gathering a dropped ball from Smith to sprint under the posts, Griffiths adding the goal to clinch a match still talked about to this day.

Match statistics:
Wigan 19 St Helens 14
Northern Rugby League Championship
Friday 27 March 1959 at Central Park, Wigan (kick-off: 3.00 p.m.)

Wigan	**St Helens**
(blue with white bands)	(white with red band)

Full-back:

Fred Griffiths (5 goals)	Glyn Moses

Three-quarters:

Billy Boston (try)	Tom van Vollenhoven
Eric Ashton (captain, try)	Duggie Greenall (captain, try)
Keith Holden, Mick Sullivan	Brian Howard, Jan Prinsloo (try)

Half-backs:

David Bolton	Alex Murphy (try)
Rees Thomas	Wilf Smith (try)

Forwards:

Bill Bretherton, Bill Sayer,	Derek Brown (goal), Eddie
Brian McTigue,	Bowden, Brian Briggs,
Norman Cherrington,	Fred Terry, Dick Huddart,
Don Platt, Roy Evans (try)	Vince Karalius

Coach:

Joe Egan	*Coach:* Jim Sullivan

Referee: Eric Clay (Leeds)
Attendance: 47,747
Weather: Overcast, strong wind, damp conditions

Half-time: 9-0
Receipts: £4,804

First half:

7 min.	Griffiths (Wigan)	penalty	2-0
20 min.	Griffiths (Wigan)	penalty	4-0
24 min.	Evans (Wigan)	try	7-0
	Griffiths (Wigan)	conversion	9-0

Second half:

55 min.	Boston (Wigan)	try	12-0
	Griffiths (Wigan)	conversion	14-0
63 min.	Murphy (St Helens)	try	14-3
68 min.	Smith (St Helens)	try	14-6
	Brown (St Helens)	conversion	14-8
73 min.	Ashton (Wigan)	try	17-8
	Griffiths (Wigan)	conversion	19-8
74 min.	Greenall (St Helens)	try	19-11
78 min.	Prinsloo (St Helens)	try	19-14

WIGAN v. HULL Rugby League Challenge Cup final
9 May 1959, Wembley Stadium, London

Wigan became the first club to grace the Wembley turf six times when they took on Hull in the 1959 Challenge Cup decider. Wigan were virtually at full strength, the only doubt having been skipper Eric Ashton, who required a painkilling injection in his leg beforehand. The Humbersiders, making their debut in front of the famous Twin Towers, had ridden the rocky route to Wembley on the back of a fearsome pack, four of whom represented Great Britain during their careers. In the event, they appeared to freeze on the big day, allowing Wigan to take control and rack up a record Wembley score in the process.

After just eight minutes Ashton broke through Hull's defence, feeding co-centre Keith Holden, who sidestepped Brian Cooper and Arthur Keegan to go under the posts, Fred Griffiths adding a simple conversion. Minutes later a long-range penalty from Keegan reduced the margin to three points but it did not last long, Wigan scoring two spellbinding length-of-the-field tries. First, Mick Sullivan raced 75 yards to score in the corner after Hull lost the ball near the Wigan line, David Bolton picking up before beating two defenders and despatching a wide scoring pass to the left-winger. Bolton himself then covered 60 yards, placing the ball under the posts following a surging run from Brian McTigue. Griffiths added both goals, the first going in off the post, placing Wigan safely ahead 15-2 after 30 minutes. Keegan added a second Hull penalty before Billy Boston scored Wigan's fourth try, racing 20 yards to crash over in the corner, an excellent Griffiths goal making it 20-4 at half-time.

Stan Cowan looked as though he might score Hull's first touchdown after the interval, but passed inside when he appeared to have a better chance going for the line himself. Meanwhile, Wigan had two efforts by John Barton and Holden disallowed. It was left to the trusty boot of Keegan to open the second-half scoring, his two penalties bringing Hull to within twelve points. Tries by eventual Lance Todd winner McTigue and Boston (following up a Bolton kick-through), Griffiths converting the former, put the match out of Hull's reach at 28-8. With eight minutes left, Finn scored the Airlie Birds' only try, Keegan tagging on his fifth goal before Griffiths completed a good afternoon's work with a long-range penalty.

Lance Todd Trophy winner Brian McTigue places the ball over the line for his 60th-minute try.

It was reported the men from Central Park were offered pep pills before the game but refused. They certainly did not need them, providing an exciting exhibition of rugby skills to retain the trophy in style.

Match statistics:
Wigan 30 Hull 13
Rugby League Challenge Cup final
Saturday 9 May 1959 at Wembley Stadium, London (kick-off: 3.00 p.m.)

Wigan	*Hull*
(cherry and white hoops)	(white with black V)

Full-back:
Fred Griffiths (6 goals)   Arthur Keegan (5 goals)

Three-quarters:
Billy Boston (2 tries)   Stan Cowan
Eric Ashton (captain)   Brian Cooper
Keith Holden (try)   Brian Saville
Mick Sullivan (try)   Ivor Watts

Half-backs:
David Bolton (try)   George Matthews
Rees Thomas   Tommy Finn (try)

Forwards:
Bill Bretherton, Bill Sayer,   Mike Scott, Tommy Harris,
John Barton, Brian McTigue (try),   Jim Drake, Cyril Sykes, Bill Drake,
Norman Cherrington, Roy Evans   Johnny Whiteley (captain)

Coach: *Coach:*
Joe Egan   Roy Francis

Referee: Charlie Appleton (Warrington)   *Half-time:* 20-4
Attendance: 79,811   *Receipts:* £35,718
Weather: Sunny and cloudy

First half:

8 min.	Holden (Wigan)	try	3-0
	Griffiths (Wigan)	conversion	5-0
12 min.	Keegan (Hull)	penalty	5-2
22 min.	Sullivan (Wigan)	try	8-2
	Griffiths (Wigan)	conversion	10-2
30 min.	Bolton (Wigan)	try	13-2
	Griffiths (Wigan)	conversion	15-2
32 min.	Keegan (Hull)	penalty	15-4
35 min.	Boston (Wigan)	try	18-4
	Griffiths (Wigan)	conversion	20-4

Second half:

49 min.	Keegan (Hull)	penalty	20-6
58 min.	Keegan (Hull)	penalty	20-8
60 min.	McTigue (Wigan)	try	23-8
	Griffiths (Wigan)	conversion	25-8
70 min.	Boston (Wigan)	try	28-8
72 min.	Finn (Hull)	try	28-11
	Keegan (Hull)	conversion	28-13
78 min.	Griffiths (Wigan)	penalty	30-13

WIGAN v. LEEDS Rugby League Challenge Cup round two
27 February 1960, Central Park, Wigan

This tense Challenge Cup tie was described as 'one of the most hectic and thrilling finishes ever seen at Central Park.' For the Wigan fans, Mick Sullivan was the hero, as his last-gasp try 'took Wigan from the jaws of defeat' with slightly over one minute remaining and Leeds two points ahead. Many home supporters among the massive 33,000 crowd were already leaving, but, as the *Wigan Observer* noted, they missed 'a never to be forgotten end.'

The architect was Brian McTigue. From an innocuous play-the-ball in midfield, the alert McTigue, realising there was space to his left, delivered a pass that instigated a move eagerly continued by halves Terry Entwhistle and David Bolton. The latter fed the ball to Sullivan, who raced for the corner as Gordon Brown, Derek Hallas and Barry Simms desperately tried to get across and block his route. It was to no avail, as the winger crossed the line a yard from the corner flag, the Central Park ground exploding into a wall of sound. Fred Griffiths sealed the win at 14-11 with an excellent touchline conversion, Wigan keeping on course to be the first side to win three successive Wembley finals (They lost at Hull in the next tie).

In truth, the Cherry and Whites appeared to have control of the outcome in the first half, taking an early 7-0 lead. Leeds, inspired by Lewis Jones, clawed their way back and looked all set for a famous victory. Jones, the former 'Golden Boy' of Welsh Rugby Union who joined Leeds in 1952, was highly praised by the Wigan press for his display. In the second half his immaculate touch-finding, aided by a strong wind and gaining distances of up to 75 yards, continually kept Wigan penned into their own 25. In fact, match-winner Sullivan and full-back Griffiths had spent most of the half defending against them on the touchlines.

Centre Keith Holden had opened the scoring in the sixth minute, cutting inside the Leeds defence after taking a pass from Griffiths, who also converted.

Two of the match heroes – Mick Sullivan (left), who produced the winner for Wigan, and Leeds' Lewis Jones (from a 1961 caricature), who was outstanding in defeat.

Griffiths and Jones then registered two penalties apiece, pushing Wigan ahead 9-4 at the break. Another Jones penalty after the resumption narrowed the gap to three points, triggering a strong Leeds offensive, Fred Pickup grabbing the Loiners' first try just ten minutes later. Inevitably, Jones was the creator with a short kick that Pickup seized upon, dummying to wing-partner Eddie Ratcliffe before outwitting Entwhistle and Billy Boston to score in the corner. Jones' touchline kick put Leeds ahead for the first time at 11-9. The Yorkshiremen then spent some 24 minutes stoutly defending before Sullivan's 'grandstand finish'.

Match statistics:
Wigan 14 Leeds 11
Rugby League Challenge Cup round two
Saturday 27 February 1960 at Central Park, Wigan (kick-off: 3.00 p.m.)

Wigan	*Leeds*
(cherry and white hoops)	(blue with amber bands)

Full-back:	
Fred Griffiths (4 goals)	Gordon Brown

Three-quarters:	
Billy Boston	Del Hodgkinson
Eric Ashton (captain)	Derek Hallas
Keith Holden (try)	Fred Pickup (try)
Mick Sullivan (try)	Eddie Ratcliffe

Half-backs:	
David Bolton	Lewis Jones (captain, 4 goals)
Terry Entwhistle	Colin Evans

Forwards:	
John Barton, Bill Sayer,	Jack Fairbank, Barry Simms,
Frank Collier, Norman Cherrington,	Colin Tomlinson, Don Robinson,
Brian McTigue, Jack Gregory	John Sewell, Dennis Goodwin

Coach:
Joe Egan

Referee: Ron Gelder (Wilmslow)   Half-time: 9-4
Attendance: 33,388   Receipts: £4,009
Weather: Cloudy, very windy

First half:

6 min.	Holden (Wigan)	try	3-0
	Griffiths (Wigan)	conversion	5-0
18 min.	Griffiths (Wigan)	penalty	7-0
— min.	Jones (Leeds)	penalty	7-2
— min.	Jones (Leeds)	penalty	7-4
— min.	Griffiths (Wigan)	penalty	9-4

Second half:

45 min.	Jones (Leeds)	penalty	9-6
55 min.	Pickup (Leeds)	try	9-9
	Jones (Leeds)	conversion	9-11
79 min.	Sullivan (Wigan)	try	12-11
	Griffiths (Wigan)	conversion	14-11

Wigan v. Wakefield Trinity Northern Rugby League
Championship final, 21 May 1960, Odsal Stadium, Bradford

The 1960 Championship final at Odsal attracted Britain's second-highest attendance (after the 1954 Challenge Cup final replay at the same venue) outside of Wembley. The 83,000-plus crowd was relishing the prospect of Wigan taking on a Wakefield Trinity side brimming with confidence after the previous week's 38-5 Challenge Cup final blitz over Hull.

Wigan were handicapped by the suspension of winger Mick Sullivan following an altercation with Alex Murphy in the play-off semi-final. He had played in the unaccustomed role of stand-off in that match with regular 'number six' David Bolton at scrum-half. Wigan's back division retained its irregular look for the final, Bolton continuing at scrum-half with skipper Eric Ashton as his half-back partner and Billy Boston taking Ashton's place in the centre. Frank Halliwell filled Boston's right wing berth while Syd Fenton – normally a half-back – continued his recent run at left-wing. In another surprise, regular prop Brian McTigue moved to the second row, exchanging places with Frank Collier.

In the tension-filled atmosphere, Wigan, either through nerves or the many positional changes, were not at their best in the first half. Nonetheless, they went in at the interval 9-3 ahead, having overcome a Wakefield try from Fred Smith after two minutes, when he took a pass from Ken Rollin, the stand-off having made a lengthy downfield run following a Don Vines burst. Two successful penalties by Fred Griffiths nosed Wigan 4-3 ahead before Boston, with half-time beckoning, wrong-footed Trinity full-back Gerry Round, going outside him to score near the flag, Griffiths adding an excellent third goal.

Wakefield – handicapped by a 12th-minute injury to influential centre Neil Fox, who then spent the match limping on the left flank – looked a tired team in the

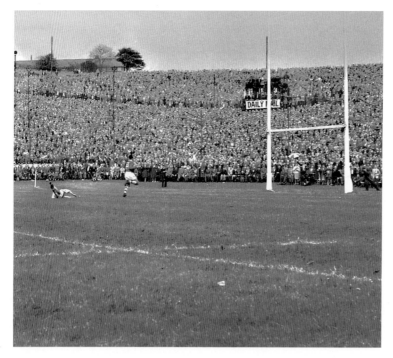

Billy Boston leaves a Wakefield defender clutching thin air as he races towards the posts for his second try following an interception watched by the massive Odsal crowd.

second half. Wigan's pack, led by rampaging runs from John Barton, Collier and McTigue, took control. Ashton scored the try that broke Wakefield's resolve 11 minutes into the second period when, kicking over Round, he recovered the ball to dive over. Griffiths missed the goal but added a penalty minutes later for a 14-3 lead. With an hour gone, Bill Sayer added another try, racing over from acting half-back despite the attentions of Derek Turner. Six minutes later, Boston intercepted a Len Chamberlain pass at the halfway line to race away virtually unopposed. Ashton crowned an excellent personal display when, having received a Bolton pass from a scrum 35 yards out he evaded Round for the final points of the day. Although Wakefield lost convincingly at 27-3, they had the courageous Round to thank for preventing the ever-dangerous Boston from adding a possible four more tries!

Match statistics:
Wigan 27 Wakefield Trinity 3
Northern Rugby League Championship final
Saturday 21 May 1960 at Odsal Stadium, Bradford (kick-off: 3.00 p.m.)

Wigan	**Wakefield Trinity**
(red)	(white)

Full-back:
Fred Griffiths (6 goals)   Gerry Round

Three-quarters:
Frank Halliwell, Billy Boston (2 tries),   Fred Smith (try), Alan Skene,
Keith Holden, Syd Fenton   Neil Fox, John Etty

Half-backs:
Eric Ashton (captain, 2 tries)   Ken Rollin
David Bolton   Keith Holliday

Forwards:
John Barton, Bill Sayer (try),   Jack Wilkinson, Geoff Oakes,
Frank Collier, Brian McTigue,   Don Vines, Albert Firth,
Geoff Lyon, Roy Evans   Len Chamberlain, Derek Turner (captain)

Coach: *Coach:*
Joe Egan   Ken Traill

Referee: Eric Clay (Leeds)   *Half-time:* 9-3
Attendance: 83,190   *Receipts:* £14,482
Weather: Dry and warm

First half:

2 min.	Smith (Wakefield Trinity)	try	0-3
8 min.	Griffiths (Wigan)	penalty	2-3
22 min.	Griffiths (Wigan)	penalty	4-3
39 min.	Boston (Wigan)	try	7-3
	Griffiths (Wigan)	conversion	9-3

Second half:

51 min.	Ashton (Wigan)	try	12-3
56 min.	Griffiths (Wigan)	penalty	14-3
61 min.	Sayer (Wigan)	try	17-3
	Griffiths (Wigan)	conversion	19-3
67 min.	Boston (Wigan)	try	22-3
	Griffiths (Wigan)	conversion	24-3
77 min.	Ashton (Wigan)	try	27-3

WIGAN v. HUNSLET Rugby League Challenge Cup final
8 May 1965, Wembley Stadium, London

This match was acclaimed, at the time, as the most exciting Wembley Challenge Cup final ever. Surprise finalists Hunslet were not expected to trouble the Cherry and Whites but, playing like men inspired, they gave Wigan a real battle and contributed to a memorable match. Although this was Wigan's fifth final since 1958, they had eight players making their Wembley debut, the team going through a rebuilding programme under player/coach Eric Ashton. In addition to the famous trio of Ashton, Billy Boston and Brian McTigue, only Keith Holden and Roy Evans had sampled its unique atmosphere before.

With only fifty-four seconds gone, Laurie Gilfedder registered what was then the quickest score in a Wembley final, landing a penalty from the centre spot after Hunslet's Alan Marchant had sent the ball directly out of play from kick-off. Unflustered, Hunslet were soon level through a Billy Langton goal from 45 yards after Evans was penalised for grabbing Bernard Prior's jersey as he went for a loose ball. In the 13th minute the Yorkshire side almost took a sensational lead when John Griffiths, capitalising on an overlap created by a Fred Ward 'dummy', dived in near the right corner flag. The touch judge, however, controversially ruled Griffiths was pushed into touch-in-goal by Trevor Lake. Hunslet's Brian Gabbitas later said: 'That disallowed try really sank us. We would have had our noses in front and would have kept them there.'

Minutes later Wigan struck when Langton failed to find touch from a penalty, Gilfedder and Ray Ashby creating room on the right and, with Hunslet's defence

Keith Holden dives over for Wigan's first try as he evades Hunslet's Brian Gabbitas and Barry Lee (far right).

Joint Lance Todd Trophy winner Ray Ashby makes another telling break for Wigan.

concentrated on the dangerous Ashton–Boston duo, Holden burst through the inside channel to score a great try. Penalty goals from Langton and Gilfedder pushed the score to 7-4 for Wigan. The game was now flowing, with Wigan moving the ball well, their threat increased with the constant linking up on attack by full-back Ashby. Hunslet were also showing enterprise, although Wigan appeared to have the game 'in the bag' when Lake scored after being put through by Holden, rounding the defence to place the ball midway between corner flag and post, Gilfedder adding the goal. Hunslet refused to lie down and Gabbitas – having a sensational game that would earn him a share of the Lance Todd Trophy with the equalling outstanding Ashby – sent centre Geoff Shelton scorching in under the posts as he evaded four defenders. Langton's goal meant that, at 12-9 down, the Leeds-based side was very much in contention as the interval whistle sounded.

The second half opened fortuitously for Wigan when Hunslet lost the ball when mounting a strong attack, McTigue and Evans combining to send Gilfedder on a 45-yard chase to the line, resisting Shelton and Langton to score in the corner. Ashton, taking over from a breathless Gilfedder, produced an excellent touchline conversion. Holden had a try under the posts disallowed, being penalised for a 'double movement' while, at the other end, Langton missed an easy penalty chance. Midway through the half Hunslet began exerting terrific pressure on the Wigan line, three try-threatening chances being lost through poor passes within as many minutes. Moments after the final error they were made to pay, as Ashby, from just inside Wigan's 25, squeezed past three defenders to sprint some 30 yards towards the left, feeding Lake at the halfway line. A thrilling chase to the corner ended with the Rhodesian flyer escaping Griffiths' despairing tackle to dive over for one of the most spectacular touchdowns seen at Wembley. Gilfedder was unable to add the

Back-row forward
Roy Evans at
Wembley for the
fourth time
with Wigan.

extras and missed a straightforward penalty shortly after but, with a 20-9 lead and under 20 minutes to play, it seemed a safe bet the trophy was heading for Central Park. Hunslet had other ideas and, inspired by second-rowers Geoff Gunney and Bill Ramsey, their pack began to fire on all cylinders, the reward coming when Griffiths finally got his try, racing straight under the posts as he avoided four defenders. Langton converted and added a penalty with four minutes remaining to make the score 20-16. Hunslet were now on top, but Wigan held on for a memorable win. The *Wigan Observer* commented that 'Wigan were matched step for step by Hunslet, who not only rose to the occasion but soared high above it.'

Match statistics:
Wigan 20 Hunslet 16
Rugby League Challenge Cup final
Saturday 8 May 1965 at Wembley Stadium, London (kick-off: 3.00 p.m.)

Wigan	*Hunslet*
(cherry and white hoops)	(white with chocolate V)

Full-back:
Ray Ashby   Billy Langton (5 goals)

Three-quarters:
Billy Boston   John Griffiths (try)
Eric Ashton (captain, goal)   Geoff Shelton (try)
Keith Holden (try)   Alan Preece
Trevor Lake (2 tries)   Barry Lee

Half-backs:
Cliff Hill   Brian Gabbitas
Frank Parr   Alan Marchant

Forwards:
Danny Gardiner, Colin Clarke   Dennis Hartley, Bernard Prior,
Brian McTigue, Tony Stephens,   Ken Eyre, Bill Ramsey,
Roy Evans, Laurie Gilfedder   Geoff Gunney, Fred Ward
(try, 3 goals)   (captain)

Substitutes:
Kevin O'Loughlin (did not play)   Arthur Render (did not play)
Geoff Lyon (did not play)   Billy Baldwinson (did not play)

Player/coach: *Player/coach:*
Eric Ashton   Fred Ward

Referee: Joe Manley (Warrington)   *Half-time:* 12-9
Attendance: 89,016   *Receipts:* £48,080
Weather: Sunny and warm

First half:

1 min.	Gilfedder (Wigan)	penalty	2-0
4 min.	Langton (Hunslet)	penalty	2-2
16 min.	Holden (Wigan)	try	5-2
25 min.	Langton (Hunslet)	penalty	5-4
30 min.	Gilfedder (Wigan)	penalty	7-4
33 min.	Lake (Wigan)	try	10-4
	Gilfedder (Wigan)	conversion	12-4
38 min.	Shelton (Hunslet)	try	12-7
	Langton (Hunslet)	conversion	12-9

Second half:

44 min.	Glifedder (Wigan)	try	15-9
	Ashton (Wigan)	conversion	17-9
59 min.	Lake (Wigan)	try	20-9
65 min.	Griffiths (Hunslet)	try	20-12
	Langton (Hunslet)	conversion	20-14
76 min.	Langton (Hunslet)	penalty	20-16

WIGAN v. ST HELENS Northern Rugby League Championship final
22 May 1971, Station Road, Swinton

From a Wigan perspective, this was certainly 'the one that got away', losing a Championship final that had one of the most sensational and controversial finishes ever. One journalist commented: 'If justice had been done, the trophy would be in the Wigan boardroom. Wigan, the better team for 75 minutes, released their grip and had the match snatched from them.' Wigan, who led the 1970/71 League table with just four defeats, two points clear of St Helens, were going through a transitional period as coach Eric Ashton sought to rebuild the side. The old guard of Billy Boston, Brian McTigue and Ashton himself had retired, and new heroes – particularly Wigan's influential back three of Bill Ashurst, Dave Robinson and Doug Laughton – were making their presence felt.

St Helens went in at the interval leading 6-3, although most scribes took the view that Wigan had outplayed their opposition for much of the first period, registering the half's only try through Robinson, a wonderful eighth-minute effort created by a perfect defence-splitting pass from Ashurst. A crucial factor was that, whereas Colin Tyrer missed four reasonable first-half goal chances, Saints skipper Kel Coslett landed three (two penalties and a drop goal). Several pundits, believing Tyrer was not 100 per cent having 'passed' a fitness test on a groin the day before, suggested the responsibility should have passed to Ashurst.

With a strong wind behind them in the second half, Wigan turned their superiority into points when Ashurst, who 'gave one of the finest all-round displays of back-row forward work seen for many a match', dived between the posts two minutes after the restart. Tyrer's conversion, plus two well-taken Ashurst drop goals, put Wigan ahead 12-6. When John Mantle was dismissed seven minutes from time, reportedly for kicking Ashurst, it should have made the result safe. Instead, twelve-man St Helens threw caution to the wind, Coslett saying later: 'We knew we had to pull out something extra and that is when we started to play the fast, open rugby

One that got away! Wigan scrum-half Warren Ayres is held short of the try-line by St Helens duo Eric Chisnall (left) and Jeff Heaton during a first-half incident.

that eventually won the match for us.' Four minutes from time, St Helens swept the ball to the left for Bob Blackwood to score in the corner. Coslett, with a great touchline kick, closed the margin to 12-11. With a minute left the moment of dispute arrived. Saints' John Walsh attempted a drop goal, his miscued kick veering towards the corner flag. The bounce beat Wigan's Stuart Wright as Billy Benyon plucked the ball out of the air to score, Coslett converting. Ashton claimed: 'Benyon could never have got to the ball so fast' but referee Eric Lawrinson clearly disagreed!

Match statistics:
Wigan 12 St Helens 16
Northern Rugby League Championship final
Saturday 22 May 1971 at Station Road, Swinton (kick-off: 3.00 p.m.)

Wigan	**St Helens**
(cherry and white hoops)	(white with red V)

Full-back:
Colin Tyrer (goal)　　　　　　　　　　　　Geoff Pimblett

Three-quarters:
Kevin O'Loughlin, Bill Francis,　　　　　Les Jones, Billy Benyon (try),
Peter Rowe, Stuart Wright　　　　　　　John Walsh,
　　　　　　　　　　　　　　　　　　　　　Bob Blackwood (try)

Half-backs:
David Hill, Warren Ayres　　　　　　　　Alan Whittle, Jeff Heaton

Forwards:
Brian Hogan, Colin Clarke,　　　　　　　John Stephens, Tony Karalius,
Geoff Fletcher, Bill Ashurst (try, 2 goals),　Graham Rees, John Mantle,
Dave Robinson (try),　　　　　　　　　　Eric Chisnall, Kel Coslett
Doug Laughton (captain)　　　　　　　　(captain, 5 goals)

Substitutes:
Eddie Cunningham for Robinson 46 min.　Bob Wanbon for Rees 40 min.
David Gandy (did not play)　　　　　　　Ken Kelly for Benyon 80 min.

Team manager:　　　　　　　　　　　　*Team manager:*
Eric Ashton　　　　　　　　　　　　　　Jim Challinor

Referee: Eric Lawrinson (Warrington)　　*Half-time:* 3-6
Attendance: 21,745　　　　　　　　　　*Receipts:* £10,201
Weather: Sunny and warm

First half:

8 min.	Robinson (Wigan)	try	3-0
10 min.	Coslett (St Helens)	penalty	3-2
— min.	Coslett (St Helens)	drop goal	3-4
— min.	Coslett (St Helens)	penalty	3-6

Second half:

42 min.	Ashurst (Wigan)	try	6-6
	Tyrer (Wigan)	conversion	8-6
— min.	Ashurst (Wigan)	drop goal	10-6
70 min.	Ashurst (Wigan)	drop goal	12-6
76 min.	Blackwood (St Helens)	try	12-9
	Coslett (St Helens)	conversion	12-11
79 min.	Benyon (St Helens)	try	12-14
	Coslett (St Helens)	conversion	12-16

WIGAN v. LEEDS John Player Trophy final
22 January 1983, Elland Road, Leeds

Leeds United AFC's Elland Road ground on a damp January day in 1983 was the unlikely scene of an important landmark in the history of the Wigan club. The fact that it was the first success for the Cherry and Whites in the John Player Trophy, inaugurated in 1971/72, was irrelevant. What really counted was that it gave vindication and impetus to the ambition of 'The Gang of Four' – the four-man board, of which Maurice Lindsay was a pivotal figure, that had taken over the club affairs in 1982. It was Wigan's first silverware since winning the Lancashire Cup in 1973 and appeared to justify the appointment of Alex Murphy as coach the previous June. Lindsay said after the game: 'Here's hoping that this is going to be the start of something big.' He could never have imagined just how 'big' that 'something' would be over the coming years!

The first half was not particularly inspiring from either side, a drop goal and penalty from Wigan skipper Colin Whitfield being matched by two penalties from Leeds' Kevin Dick. The second half saw a more determined Wigan take the field, boosted by tremendous vocal support from their fans and Murphy's strongly worded interval team talk! After an early second-half scare when Leeds' Les Dyl was held on his back over the Wigan try-line, the Lancashire team began to assert itself. This was particularly true after Murphy substituted an 'out-of-sorts' Graeme West with Brian Case, a move that seemed to lift the Wigan pack.

The game turned in the 57th minute, when David Stephenson engineered an opening for Henderson Gill, who just managed to squeeze past three defenders to go over in the corner, being injured in the process. Whitfield's touchline conversion gave his side a real boost, although the score, at 8-4, still appeared too close to call. Whitfield stretched the gap with a penalty and Wigan began to control the final with some excellent rugby in the difficult conditions. Dennis Ramsdale, Danny Campbell and Case all went close to crossing the Leeds line before Mick Scott settled matters when his break sent in Brian Juliff – who had replaced the beleaguered Gill – to score behind the posts. Whitfield's goal completed the scoring

Post-match celebrations! From left to right, standing: David Stephenson, Keith Mills (physiotherapist), Brian Juliff, Brian Case, Danny Campbell, Glyn Shaw, Barry Williams, Mick Scott, Graeme West. Kneeling: Henderson Gill, John Pendlebury, Martin Foy, Colin Whitfield (captain, with trophy), Nicky Kiss, Jimmy Fairhurst, Dennis Ramsdale.

and the £10,000 winners cheque was Central Park-bound! Whitfield, who played most of the match with the discomfort of a broken nose, said afterwards: 'Our fans were magic. As soon as we ran down the tunnel (for the second half) it was incredible the way they lifted us straight away.'

Match statistics:
Wigan 15 Leeds 4
John Player Trophy final
Saturday 22 January 1983 at Elland Road, Leeds (kick-off: 2.15 p.m.)

Wigan	**Leeds**
(cherry and white hoops)	(blue with amber bands)
Full-back:	
Barry Williams	Neil Hague
Three-quarters:	
Dennis Ramsdale	Mark Campbell
David Stephenson	Ian Wilkinson
Colin Whitfield (captain, 4 goals, drop goal)	Les Dyl
Henderson Gill (try)	Andy Smith
Half-backs:	
Martin Foy	John Holmes
Jimmy Fairhurst	Kevin Dick (2 goals)
Forwards:	
Glyn Shaw	Roy Dickinson
Nicky Kiss	David Ward (captain)
Danny Campbell	Tony Burke
Graeme West	Andy Sykes
Mick Scott	Wayne Heron
John Pendlebury	David Heron
Substitutes:	
Brian Case for West 50 min.	Mark Conway (did not play)
Brian Juliff (try) for Gill 57 min.	David Heselwood (did not play)
Coach:	*Coach:*
Alex Murphy	Robin Dewhurst

Referee: Ron Campbell (Widnes)
Attendance: 19,553
Weather: Overcast and damp

Half-time: 3-4
Receipts: £49,027

First half:

7 min.	Whitfield (Wigan)	drop goal	1-0
11 min.	Dick (Leeds)	penalty	1-2
33 min.	Dick (Leeds)	penalty	1-4
34 min.	Whitfield (Wigan)	penalty	3-4

Second half:

57 min.	Gill (Wigan)	try	6-4
	Whitfield (Wigan)	conversion	8-4
64 min.	Whitfield (Wigan)	penalty	10-4
75 min.	Juliff (Wigan)	try	13-4
	Whitfield (Wigan)	conversion	15-4

WIGAN v. HULL Rugby League Challenge Cup final
4 May 1985, Wembley Stadium, London

The 1985 Rugby League Challenge Cup final is generally considered the most outstanding ever staged at Wembley. The ten-try feast certainly caught the imagination of the BBC, who repeated it several times that year and even did a Christmas 'special'! The match had so much to savour, it is difficult to know where to start eulogising. One reporter accurately summed it all up when he said: 'Rarely, if ever, can a major sporting event have lived up to the high-pressure publicity as vividly as this one did. It had everything. Nothing was missing from the seemingly bottomless pit of spills and thrills.' Nearly every try – for winner and loser – was a classic, with Hull playing a full part. Rarely can a team have performed as well in the stadium as they did and still lose.

In an era when it was not unusual for clubs to fly Australian players, who had had to return home around February for their own competition, halfway across the planet to take part in the big day, the money can never have been better spent. Stand-off Brett Kenny – the first Australian to claim the Lance Todd Man of the Match award – and wingman John Ferguson had massive games for Wigan, as did their fellow countryman Peter Sterling – Kenny's half-back partner 'Down Under' at Parramatta – who played outstandingly in Hull's colours.

It was the men in the famous irregular black and white hoops that drew first blood when Welsh wing Kevin James scored in the right corner adding to an early penalty by Hull skipper Lee Crooks to lead 6-0 after 11 minutes. Six minutes later Wigan were level when Ferguson, with a try orchestrated by Kenny and Ian Potter, scored

John Ferguson evades Hull's Fred Ah Kuoi as he scores the opening Wigan try.

Wigan's Ian Potter feels the full weight of Hull's Neil Puckering as Nicky Kiss looks on (far right).

near the corner flag, Henderson Gill adding a superb touchline conversion to tie the score at 6-6. Kenny – who had looked so laid-back during the pre-match presentation that he appeared almost disinterested in proceedings – electrified the near-98,000 attendance ten minutes later with one of the most brilliant solo efforts seen at Wembley. Taking a long pass from young scrum-half partner Mike Ford, he accelerated with deceptive pace in an arc that took him past Gary Kemble to touch down. David Stephenson's conversion put Wigan 12-6 ahead, giving them a lead they would retain for the rest of the game.

After Crooks had landed a second penalty, Gill scored one of the most memorable tries of the afternoon after he was sent haring down the left flank following a quick passing movement involving Ford, Kenny and Stephenson. Hugging the touchline, he outpaced Kemble to score in the left corner, his beaming smile as he looked up appearing in many of the following morning's sports pages.

Three minutes after the interval, Ford and Kenny combined from a scrum – following a James knock-on in his own 25 – in front of the Hull posts. A young Shaun Edwards was quickly up in support– a trait that featured throughout his career – to take Kenny's pass and touch down behind the posts. Gill's extra points made the score 22-8.

It was 'never-say-die' Sterling who gave Hull's fans a glimmer of hope when he sent Steve Evans in at the corner minutes later but, when Ferguson recovered a loose ball to scorch over for his second try, Gill adding a difficult touchline kick, it looked all over. With the score at 28-12 and less than 30 minutes remaining, the Wigan supporters around the ground must have felt the cup was as good as won

WIGAN v. HULL

Lance Todd Trophy winner Brett Kenny heads for the try-line in the 27th minute to put Wigan ahead for the first time.

Wigan skipper Graeme West in the thick of the action tries to make ground despite the combined effort of two Hull defenders.

but, like Hunslet twenty years earlier, Hull refused to lie down and staged a magnificent, gutsy fightback.

Three tries – two excellent efforts from James Leuluai and another from substitute Gary Divorty – brought Hull back into contention in a nail-biting finish. Thankfully for Wigan, all three conversions failed, but Hull were within four points and, with a few minutes remaining on the clock, looked dangerous. One last Hull attack saw Evans brought down as he threatened on the left. The final hooter can never have been a more welcome sound. Relieved Wigan skipper Graeme West said afterwards: 'It was one of the greatest sporting occasions of my life and a great team effort.'

Match statistics:
Wigan 28 Hull 24
Rugby League Challenge Cup final
Saturday 4 May 1985 at Wembley Stadium, London (kick-off: 3.00 p.m.)

Wigan	*Hull*
(cherry and white hoops)	(black and white irregular hoops)

Full-back:

Shaun Edwards (try)	Gary Kemble

Three-quarters:

John Ferguson (2 tries)	Kevin James (try)
David Stephenson (goal)	Steve Evans (try)
Steve Donlan	James Leuluai (2 tries)
Henderson Gill (try, 3 goals)	Dane O'Hara

Half-backs:

Brett Kenny (try), Mike Ford	Fred Ah Kuoi, Peter Sterling

Forwards:

Neil Courtney, Nicky Kiss,	Lee Crooks (captain, 2 goals),
Brian Case, Graeme West (captain),	Shaun Patrick, Neil Puckering,
Brian Dunn, Ian Potter	John Muggleton, Paul Rose,
	Steve Norton

Substitutes:

Danny Campbell for Case 55 min.	Garry Schofield for O'Hara 58 min.
Nick du Toit (did not play)	Gary Divorty (try) for Puckering 58 min.

Coaches:	*Team manager:*
Colin Clarke and Alan McInnes	Arthur Bunting

Referee: Ron Campbell (Widnes)	*Half-time:* 16-8
Attendance: 97,801	*Receipts:* £760,322
Weather: Sunny and warm	

First half:

2 min.	Crooks (Hull)	penalty	0-2
11 min.	James (Hull)	try	0-6
17 min.	Ferguson (Wigan)	try	4-6
	Gill (Wigan)	conversion	6-6
27 min.	Kenny (Wigan)	try	10-6
	Stephenson (Wigan)	conversion	12-6
33 min.	Crooks (Hull)	penalty	12-8
39 min.	Gill (Wigan)	try	16-8

Second half:

43 min.	Edwards (Wigan)	try	20-8
	Gill (Wigan)	conversion	22-8
45 min.	Evans (Hull)	try	22-12
51 min.	Ferguson (Wigan)	try	26-12
	Gill (Wigan)	conversion	28-12
64 min.	Leuluai (Hull)	try	28-16
74 min.	Divorty (Hull)	try	28-20
76 min.	Leuluai (Hull)	try	28-24

WIGAN v. AUSTRALIA tour match
12 October 1986, Central Park, Wigan

Wigan's performance against the 1986 Kangaroos gave British Rugby League real hope that, after the huge gulf that appeared during the 1982 tour, the gap in standard had closed. The eagerly anticipated fixture attracted the largest crowd to witness a club game against a touring side, the Aussies putting out an almost Test-strength line-up for the opening match of their tour.

The massive turnout was not disappointed, as the two sides produced a thrilling spectacle although Wigan were slowest out of the starting blocks. After three minutes, winger Michael O'Connor crossed with ease following a break by full-back Garry Jack to put the tourists into a quick 4-0 lead. A penalty goal from Henderson Gill (after Paul Sironen had punched Wigan's Ian Roberts) halved the margin midway through the half. It looked ominous for the home side when, during a five-minute blitz, Peter Sterling (following a brilliant break from former Wigan favourite Brett Kenny) and Noel Cleal (tackled short of the line before playing the ball forward) both scored. With O'Connor converting their efforts, the interval score of 16-2 created a sense of déjà vu, reviving thoughts of 1982.

Wigan coach Graham Lowe must have used the right words during the break, as his team played with greater resolve and belief in the second half, refusing to be distracted after Wally Lewis (escaping a double tackle from Shaun Edwards and Steve Hampson) extended the Australian lead to 20-2. It was an inspired display from scrum-half and 'Man of the Match' Mike Ford (a late replacement for injury victim Ellery Hanley) that brought Wigan storming back six minutes after Lewis' effort. Ford kicked over the defensive line and, following up, booted it beyond the isolated Royce Simmons to regather and feed Edwards who, in turn, sent Dean Bell into the left corner for Wigan's first four-pointer of the match. Lifted by the crowd, the Cherry and Whites went on the rampage, with Graeme West spurting through an opening to send Edwards on a thrilling chase for the line as he outmanoeuvred Kenny, Gill's goal making it 20-12. When Aussie wing Les Kiss ran in another try, Wigan could have been excused for throwing in the towel but were having none of it. Again, Ford was instrumental as Stephenson was halted short of the line, the visitors eventually cracking when Bell and Joe Lydon combined brilliantly to send the latter under the posts. Gill's extra points completed the scoring.

Wigan's wonderful effort was put into perspective when the Australian's completed their tour with another 100 per cent record, making a clean sweep of the Ashes series.

Wigan expose tourists' slight defensive flaw

The headline in the *Daily Telegraph* raised British hopes for home success during the remainder of the 1986 Australian tour.

Match statistics:
Wigan 18 Australia 26
Tour match
Sunday 12 October 1986 at Central Park, Wigan (kick-off: 3.00 p.m.)

Wigan	*Australia*
(cherry and white hoops)	(green with double gold V)

Full-back:	
Steve Hampson	Garry Jack

Three-quarters:	
Dean Bell (try)	Les Kiss (try)
David Stephenson	Gene Miles
Joe Lydon (try)	Brett Kenny
Henderson Gill (3 goals)	Michael O'Connor (try, 3 goals)

Half-backs:	
Shaun Edwards (try)	Wally Lewis (captain, try)
Mike Ford	Peter Sterling (try)

Forwards:	
Graeme West (captain)	Steve Roach
Martin Dermott	Royce Simmons
Brian Case	Bryan Niebling
Ian Roberts	Paul Sironen
Ian Potter	Noel Cleal (try)
Andy Goodway	Bob Lindner

Substitutes:	
Rob Louw for Dermott 50 min.	Les Davidson for Lindner 50 min.
Nick du Toit for Edwards 63 min.	Terry Lamb for Sironen 77 min.

Coach:	*Coach:*
Graham Lowe	Don Furner

Referee: John Holdsworth (Kippax)   *Half-time:* 2-16
Attendance: 30,622   *Receipts:* £91,366
Weather: Sunny

First half:

3 min.	O'Connor (Australia)	try	0-4
21 min.	Gill (Wigan)	penalty	2-4
30 min.	Sterling (Australia)	try	2-8
	O'Connor (Australia)	conversion	2-10
35 min.	Cleal (Australia)	try	2-14
	O'Connor (Australia)	conversion	2-16

Second half:

47 min.	Lewis (Australia)	try	2-20
53 min.	Bell (Wigan)	try	6-20
57 min.	Edwards (Wigan)	try	10-20
	Gill (Wigan)	conversion	12-20
62 min.	Kiss (Australia)	try	12-24
70 min.	Lydon (Wigan)	try	16-24
	Gill (Wigan)	conversion	18-24

WIGAN v. FEATHERSTONE ROVERS Rugby League Championship
5 April 1987, Central Park, Wigan

A scoreline as lopsided as 62-7 may seem an odd choice for inclusion in a series of classic matches but, as Wigan chairman Maurice Lindsay glowingly said after the game, it was viewed as 'one of the greatest days in our history'. Years later, Lindsay still recalled it as one of the outstanding moments during his time at Central Park.

The reason for the euphoria was that the result confirmed (with four matches to spare) Wigan as Rugby League champions for the first time in twenty-seven years and the tenth overall, ending the longest title famine the club had experienced. A crowd in excess of 13,000 turned up in anticipation of a carnival night and the home supporters in their midst were not disappointed. Initially, Featherstone Rovers showed they did not intend to lie down, and international scrum-half Deryck Fox landed a neat drop goal after four minutes. Wigan were in no mood to be idle, and Andy Gregory – who had an influential match with a hand in almost every one of Wigan's twelve sizzling tries – was soon carving his way through a despairing Rovers' tackle for the opening try, his first for Wigan at Central Park since transferring from Warrington three months earlier. Five minutes later skipper Ellery Hanley burst through, as only he can, to register the first of his four touchdowns incorporating his eighth hat-trick of the campaign. For Hanley it brought his tally to 21 tries in 11 matches since coach Graham Lowe – himself in his first season with Wigan – had switched him from stand-off to loose-forward. Hanley's final try count of 59 for the season left him just three short of Johnny Ring's sixty-year-old club record.

Despite having some excellent players in their side, the Rovers found themselves in the position of being 'sacrificial lambs' on the day and, with the home pack dominating, Wigan showed irresistible form. With a 34-1 interval lead, it was party time on the terraces throughout the second period. In fact, for some, it may have appeared over before the kick-off, with Rugby League Public Relations Officer David Howes being spotted entering Central Park with the Championship trophy already bedecked in Wigan colours!

Wigan completed the season with 18 consecutive victories, a run that left them fifteen points clear of St Helens in the final Championship table and brought success in the first Premiership final held at Old Trafford. Warrington – whose 'double' over Wigan inflicted their only League defeats – provided the opposition in the latter, the Cherry and Whites enjoying sweet revenge by winning 8-0.

Match statistics:
Wigan 62 Featherstone Rovers 7
Rugby League Championship
Sunday 5 April 1987 at Central Park, Wigan (kick-off: 3.00 p.m.)

Wigan	*Featherstone Rovers*
(cherry and white hoops)	(blue with narrow white hoops)

Full-back:
Steve Hampson | Chris Bibb

Three-quarters:

Henderson Gill (3 tries, goal)	David Jones
David Stephenson (try, 6 goals)	John Crossley
Dean Bell (try)	Steve Quinn (goal)
Joe Lydon (2 tries)	Paul Wild

Half-backs:

Shaun Edwards	Graham Steadman
Andy Gregory (try)	Deryck Fox (try, drop goal)

Forwards:

Brian Case	Tim Slatter
Nicky Kiss	Mark Hinchcliffe
Shaun Wane	Karl Harrison
Andy Goodway	Paul Gearey
Ian Potter	Keith Bell
Ellery Hanley (captain, 4 tries)	Peter Smith (captain)

Substitutes:

Graeme West for Wane 41 min.	Mark Campbell for Hinchcliffe 20 min.
Ray Mordt (did not play)	Nigel Barker for Quinn 66 min.

Coach: *Coach:*
Graham Lowe   Paul Daley

Referee: Robin Whitfield (Widnes)   *Half-time:* 34-1
Attendance: 13,317
Weather: Cloudy, dry conditions

First half:

4 min.	Fox (Featherstone Rovers)	drop goal	0-1
7 min.	Gregory (Wigan)	try	4-1
12 min.	Hanley (Wigan)	try	8-1
	Stephenson (Wigan)	conversion	10-1
15 min.	Gill (Wigan)	try	14-1
17 min.	Lydon (Wigan)	try	18-1
	Stephenson (Wigan)	conversion	20-1
19 min.	Hanley (Wigan)	try	24-1
	Stephenson (Wigan)	conversion	26-1
28 min.	Bell (Wigan)	try	30-1
31 min.	Gill (Wigan)	try	34-1

Second half:

42 min.	Hanley (Wigan)	try	38-1
51 min.	Lydon (Wigan)	try	42-1
	Stephenson (Wigan)	conversion	44-1
58 min.	Hanley (Wigan)	try	48-1
	Stephenson (Wigan)	conversion	50-1
62 min.	Fox (Featherstone Rovers)	try	50-5
	Quinn (Featherstone Rovers)	conversion	50-7
74 min.	Stephenson (Wigan)	try	54-7
	Stephenson (Wigan)	conversion	56-7
79 min.	Gill (Wigan)	try	60-7
	Gill (Wigan)	conversion	62-7

WIGAN v. MANLY-WARRINGAH World Club Challenge
7 October 1987, Central Park, Wigan

Having seen his team clinch their first Championship in twenty-seven years, entrepreneurial Wigan chairman Maurice Lindsay announced during April 1987: 'now we would like to play Sydney premiership winners Parramatta for the world championship. It would be a fantastic financial bonanza for both clubs if we can get the two Leagues in England and Australia to agree to it.' The match was eventually sanctioned, although when it went ahead, at Central Park six months later, Manly-Warringah had replaced Paramatta as the new Australian Premiers, having won the 1987 Grand Final on Sydney Cricket Ground just ten days earlier by 18-8 over Canberra Raiders. Lindsay got one thing right though: the £131,000 gate receipts – a Central Park record – did indeed provide the anticipated cash 'bonanza', to which was added a £20,000 winners cheque by the sponsor, Fosters.

The match, although lacking spectacular flowing rugby, was a gripping affair with defences well on top throughout. Fought out in a torrid and emotion-charged atmosphere, Manly led after only two minutes when centre Michael O'Connor's penalty punished a Wigan offside from near the posts. Amazingly, they were to be the only points scored all evening by the Aussie champions. Within minutes David Stephenson had notched a 35-yard equalizer after Manly scrum-half Des Hasler was spotted stamping on Shaun Wane by referee John Holdsworth. A 23rd-minute altercation between Shaun Edwards and Dale Shearer resulted in a second penalty strike for Stephenson, putting Wigan ahead for the first time at 4-2. It was a lead they would not lose, although just before half-time there was a scare when Manly hooker Mal Cochrane burst through, but Wigan managed to turn the supporting Shearer onto his back after he crossed the line.

A happy changing room! Graham Lowe raises the World Club Challenge Trophy as he celebrates victory with his euphoric players.

The second half opened explosively, with Stephenson adding a third penalty after Cochrane had fouled Edwards. Manly seemed unwilling to tone down their aggressive play and minutes later their second row Ron Gibbs was shown the red card after he had followed through with an elbow on Joe Lydon as the latter attempted a drop goal. Stephenson's resultant penalty was the final score of the night as Wigan held on in a frantic finish for a famous victory. To a man, the Wigan players said later they had never competed in a match played at such a furious pace.

It was an all-English triumph on the field, Wigan centre Dean Bell pulling out with a groin strain and fellow-Kiwi Graeme West a non-playing substitute. This helped to regain lost British pride after the visit of the all-conquering Australian tourists of 1982 and 1986.

Match statistics:
Wigan 8 Manly-Warringah 2
World Club Challenge
Wednesday 7 October 1987 at Central Park, Wigan (kick-off: 7.45 p.m.)

Wigan	**Manly-Warringah**
(cherry and white hoops)	(maroon with narrow white hoops)

Full-back:
Steve Hampson — Dale Shearer

Three-quarters:

Richard Russell	David Ronson
David Stephenson (4 goals)	Darrell Williams
Joe Lydon	Michael O'Connor (goal)
Henderson Gill	Stuart Davies

Half-backs:

Shaun Edwards	Cliff Lyons
Andy Gregory	Des Hasler

Forwards:

Brian Case, Nicky Kiss, Shaun Wane,	Phil Daley, Mal Cochrane, Ian Gately,
Andy Goodway, Ian Potter,	Ron Gibbs, Owen Cunningham,
Ellery Hanley (captain)	Paul Vautin (captain)

Substitutes:

Ian Lucas for Case 76 min.	Paul Shaw for Cunningham 21 min.
Ged Byrne (did not play)	Jeremy Ticehurst for Williams 54 min.
Graeme West (did not play)	Mark Brokenshire for Gately 55 min.
Ian Gildart (did not play)	Mark Pocock (did not play)

Coach: — *Coach:*
Graham Lowe — Bobby Fulton

Referee: John Holdsworth (Kippax)   *Half-time:* 4-2
Attendance: 36,895   *Receipts:* £131,000
Weather: Dry and mild

First half:

2 min.	O'Connor (Manly-W)	penalty	0-2
5 min.	Stephenson (Wigan)	penalty	2-2
23 min.	Stephenson (Wigan)	penalty	4-2

Second half:

41 min.	Stephenson (Wigan)	penalty	6-2
45 min.	Stephenson (Wigan)	penalty	8-2

Wigan v. Halifax Rugby League Challenge Cup final
30 April 1988, Wembley Stadium, London

Three years after their sensational Wembley win over Hull, Wigan returned to the Twin Towers to face Challenge Cup-holders Halifax. Once Salford had been vanquished by a semi-final record score of 34-4 on a rain-soaked Burnden Park pitch, 'cup fever' infected the Wigan public in a big way, and there was a stampede for tickets. Within hours, over 17,000 were sold at Central Park and some supporters even headed for Halifax in the hope of buying a prized ticket. Chairman Maurice Lindsay showing his usual enterprise, travelled to Wembley itself where he was somehow able to 'negotiate' an additional 500 tickets which he took back to Wigan, a move the Rugby Football League hierarchy were not happy about.

On paper, the Central Park side was a much tougher proposition than on their previous visit. Great players like Brett Kenny and John Ferguson had gone but Wigan had since recruited outstanding performers such as Dean Bell, Andy Goodway, Andy Gregory, Ellery Hanley, Kevin Iro and Joe Lydon, while Shaun Edwards had matured into an exceptional talent. Rugby League hearts went out to full-back Steve Hampson, who broke his arm seventeen days ahead of the big day in a League match with Salford at Central Park. Having already missed the Wembley experience in 1984 (broken leg) and 1985 (broken arm), Hampson took his third setback philosophically saying: 'I can cope, I am used to it by now. Somebody up there does not want me to appear at Wembley, but one day I will be there.' Even Hampson could not have realised how true that prediction would be. His destiny was to have five Wembley appearances with a Wigan side that, in 1988, was embarking on an

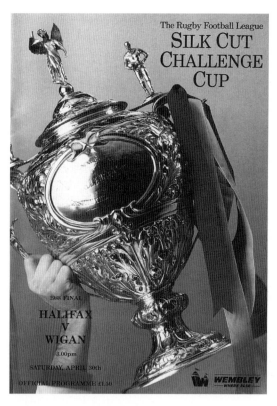

Wigan commence their historic run of eight consecutive Wembley visits.

Kevin Iro charges into the corner for his second try of the match.

unbelievable eight consecutive finals at the stadium – all of them successful! Coach Graham Lowe had wanted to rest Hampson for the Salford game but he had insisted on playing as he had, ironically, not missed a match all season.

It was not until the final 15 minutes of the opening half that Wigan finally put the first points of the game on the board with four unanswered tries before the break. Scrum-half Gregory triggered the first after 26 minutes, providing the opening for half-back partner Edwards to race half the length of the field, being tackled just a few yards short of the Halifax try-line. From the play-the-ball, powerful centre Kevin Iro ran in, forcing his way between two defenders as he went over. With the deadlock broken, Wigan piled on the agony and, four minutes later, Henderson Gill scored in the corner off a well-timed pass from Bell, Gregory having again unlocked the Halifax defence. A further Kevin Iro try followed within two minutes in the left corner, from a position created after a great burst through the middle from brother Tony. With two first-half tries against his name, expectations were raised that Kevin Iro was about to be the first to achieve a try hat-trick at Wembley, but that particular dream remained unfulfilled. On half-time, Lydon – on the end of a breathtaking move involving Gill, Bell and Edwards, with Gregory again the creator – scored the fourth near the posts. Without a recognised kicker, none of their efforts generated the extra two points, Gill, Lydon (twice) and Gregory (who hit the upright) all failing.

Six minutes after the resumption Wigan extended the lead when Tony Iro almost strolled into the right corner, picked out by a long inch-perfect pass from Gregory. This time it was Gill's turn to miss the conversion. Halifax were clearly feeling dejected at this stage – not helped by injuries to creative players Les Holliday (during the first half) and Steve Robinson (early in the second half) – and when

WIGAN v. HALIFAX

Ellery Hanley avoids the attempted tackle of Halifax wing Martin Meredith on his way to scoring the outstanding try of the final following a length-of-field break by Joe Lydon. Andy Goodway (behind Hanley) and Kevin Iro are the other prominent Wigan players.

Lydon caught the ball directly from the restart he ran 70 yards before Hanley gratefully accepted his pass to score under the posts for the try of the final. This time Gregory augmented for a 26-0 lead. Halifax finally registered their first score when player-coach Chris Anderson crossed in the corner, former Wigan player Colin Whitfield adding the conversion from the touchline. Any forlorn hope of a comeback was killed off ten minutes later when Bell – from yet another opening carved out by Gregory – touched down. This time Lydon added the goal. Although well beaten, Halifax – to their credit – came back to complete the day's scoring with one final effort when prop Neil James went over, Whitfield adding his second goal.

Wigan's emphatic 32-12 victory created history for Shaun Edwards who, at 21 years and 6 months, became the youngest ever captain at Wembley. Playing throughout with a hamstring problem (he was replaced by Ged Byrne five minutes from time) that restricted his pace he nonetheless had an excellent game. But for the want of a reliable marksman, Wigan could well have been the first side to break the forty-point barrier in a Challenge Cup final.

For Andy Gregory, whose brilliant display earned him the Lance Todd Trophy, it was his third win in four Wembley finals, the other three appearances having been with his first senior club Widnes. The delighted player said after the game: 'I was thrilled at being part of Widnes' Wembley success, but I'm a Wigan lad and today is the greatest moment in my life.'

The £1,102,247 receipts were a world record for a Rugby League match.

Match statistics:
Wigan 32 Halifax 12
Rugby League Challenge Cup final
Saturday 30 April 1988 at Wembley Stadium, London (kick-off: 3.00 p.m.)

Wigan	**Halifax**
(cherry and white hoops)	(blue and white hoops)

Full-back:
Joe Lydon (try, goal)   Graham Eadie (captain)

Three-quarters:
Tony Iro (try)   Martin Meredith
Kevin Iro (2 tries)   Chris Anderson (try)
Dean Bell (try)   Ian Wilkinson
Henderson Gill (try)   Colin Whitfield (2 goals)

Half-backs:
Shaun Edwards (captain)   Bob Grogan
Andy Gregory (goal)   Steve Robinson

Forwards:
Brian Case   Neil James (try)
Nicky Kiss   Seamus McCallion
Adrian Shelford   Keith Neller
Andy Goodway   Les Holliday
Ian Potter   Paul Dixon
Ellery Hanley (try)   John Pendlebury

Substitutes:
Ged Byrne for Edwards 75 min.   Mick Scott for Holliday 20 min.
Shaun Wane for Potter 77 min.   Dick Fairbank for Robinson 48 min.

Coach: *Player/coach:*
Graham Lowe   Chris Anderson

Referee: Fred Lindop (Wakefield)   *Half-time:* 16-0
Attendance: 94,273   *Receipts:* £1,102,247
Weather: Cloudy, slight breeze, dry

First half:

26 min.	K. Iro (Wigan)	try	4-0
30 min.	Gill (Wigan)	try	8-0
32 min.	K. Iro (Wigan)	try	12-0
39 min.	Lydon (Wigan)	try	16-0

Second half:

46 min.	T. Iro (Wigan)	try	20-0
48 min.	Hanley (Wigan)	try	24-0
	Gregory (Wigan)	conversion	26-0
55 min.	Anderson (Halifax)	try	26-4
	Whitfield (Halifax)	conversion	26-6
65 min.	Bell (Wigan)	try	30-6
	Lydon (Wigan)	conversion	32-6
68 min.	James (Halifax)	try	32-10
	Whitfield (Halifax)	conversion	32-12

Wigan v. St Helens Rugby League Challenge Cup final
29 April 1989, Wembley Stadium, London

Wigan made their fourth Wembley visit in six years and met St Helens for the third time at the famous stadium, having lost both the previous encounters with their fiercest rivals during the 1960s. St Helens had had an indifferent season – finishing midway in the League table – but could point to the fact that they had defeated Wigan 4-2 at Central Park just six days earlier in the opening round of the Premiership Trophy. The final attracted a sell-out crowd of 78,000, being the first Challenge Cup final staged at Wembley following its conversion to an all-seated stadium, which had reduced the capacity by some 20,000.

Any hopes of a tight struggle between the two teams looked a doubtful prospect as early as the first minute when seventeen-year-old Saints full-back Gary Connolly knocked on in front of his own line. Better Wembley days lay ahead for Connolly, although most of them would be in Wigan colours! The error was compounded when, in the third minute, Kevin Iro scored following sterling work by skipper Ellery Hanley, who wriggled out of a Roy Haggerty tackle before passing to the giant Kiwi. Joe Lydon just missed the kick but made amends with a penalty midway through the half. In the 26th minute, Hanley scored a try that has become one of Wembley's most enduring images. Receiving the ball from Shaun Edwards just inside the Saints half, he beat five opponents with the power and speed that was his trademark, finishing under the posts with hardly a hand placed on him. Lydon's second goal brought the score to 12-0 at half-time.

A neat Andy Gregory drop goal three minutes after the start of the second period widened the margin to thirteen points, putting early psychological pressure on St Helens, who then trailed by three scores. The Saints' misery mounted four minutes later when Kevin Iro scored his second, fleetingly raising hopes of the first Wembley hat-trick just like a year earlier. It was Gregory, however, that added the next try with 15 minutes remaining, going under the posts after supporting a terrific break down the middle by Edwards. The most popular try of all was that scored by Steve Hampson

More rejoicing as coach Graham Lowe (in blazer, centre) leads the party! The players are, from left to right, standing: Andy Platt, Ian Potter, Tony Iro, Denis Betts, Andy Goodway, Steve Hampson, Ian Lucas, Kevin Iro. Kneeling: Adrian Shelford, Nicky Kiss, Ellery Hanley (captain, with trophy), Dean Bell, Joe Lydon, Andy Gregory, Shaun Edwards.

in the final minutes, relishing his first appearance at Wembley after such atrocious luck in the past. Lydon converted Gregory's effort to make the final score 27-0.

Although the final was disappointingly one-sided as a contest, there was much to savour in Wigan's brilliant display, coach Graham Lowe commenting: 'We were in control for the full 80 minutes. Ellery Hanley was an inspirational leader.'

Match statistics:
Wigan 27 St Helens 0
Rugby League Challenge Cup final
Saturday 29 April 1989 at Wembley Stadium, London (kick-off: 3.00 p.m.)

Wigan	*St Helens*
(blue and white hoops)	(white with red V)

Full-back:
Steve Hampson (try)   Gary Connolly

Three-quarters:
Tony Iro   Michael O'Connor
Kevin Iro (2 tries)   Phil Veivers
Dean Bell   Paul Loughlin
Joe Lydon (3 goals)   Les Quirk

Half-backs:
Shaun Edwards   Shane Cooper
Andy Gregory (try, drop goal)   Neil Holding

Forwards:
Ian Lucas, Nicky Kiss,   Tony Burke, Paul Groves,
Adrian Shelford, Andy Platt,   Paul Forber, Bernard Dwyer,
Ian Potter, Ellery Hanley   Roy Haggerty, Paul Vautin
(captain, try)   (captain)

Substitutes:
Andy Goodway for Potter 66 min.   Stuart Evans for Dwyer 45 min.
Denis Betts for Kiss 72 min.   Darren Bloor for Loughlin 62 min.
                                        Dwyer for Haggerty 66 min.

Coach: *Coach:*
Graham Lowe   Alex Murphy

Referee: Ray Tennant (Castleford)   *Half-time:* 12-0
Attendance: 78,000   *Receipts:* £1,121,293
Weather: Cloudy

First half:

3 min.	K. Iro (Wigan)	try	4-0
19 min.	Lydon (Wigan)	penalty	6-0
26 min.	Hanley (Wigan)	try	10-0
	Lydon (Wigan)	conversion	12-0

Second half:

43 min.	Gregory (Wigan)	drop goal	13-0
47 min.	K. Iro (Wigan)	try	17-0
65 min.	Gregory (Wigan)	try	21-0
	Lydon (Wigan)	conversion	23-0
76 min.	Hampson (Wigan)	try	27-0

WIGAN v. ST HELENS Rugby League Challenge Cup semi-final
10 March 1990, Old Trafford, Manchester

In a semi-final tie described as a 'thriller', Wigan became only the second team to reach Wembley for a third consecutive Challenge Cup final appearance, after a sensational finish. The only Challenge Cup match played at Old Trafford to date, it produced record semi-final receipts.

It was the irrepressible skills of Wigan's loose-forward and captain Ellery Hanley that settled the game two minutes from the end, when, with the score level at 14-14, he displayed his strength and pace to burst through the St Helens defence. With the Saints' line breached, he handed the ball to the supporting Andy Goodway, who strode unopposed beneath the posts, Joe Lydon's goal sealing a 20-14 win. An elated Goodway said later: 'I have never enjoyed scoring a try more.'

It was St Helens, mindful of Wigan's big win at Wembley the previous year and the more recent 38-6 Boxing Day mauling at Central Park, who began the stronger. They took the game to Wigan from the start, but the Cherry and Whites' defence held and it was Wigan who scored first, in the tenth minute. Steve Hampson found a gap to score in the corner after good approach work by Andy Gregory and Kevin Iro. A Paul Loughlin penalty, awarded after Gregory had spoken out of turn to the referee, reduced the deficit to two points. This lifted the Saints, who scored two exciting tries before the break. The first was from scrum-half Sean Devine, who, along with half-back partner Tommy Frodsham, had been drafted in due to the long-term injuries of Neil Holding and Jonathan Griffiths. The youngster raced in under the posts, evading Martin Dermott and Iro in the process. On the stroke of half-time, hooker Paul Groves – later judged Man of the Match – sent Les Quirk off on a spectacular scoring run that covered 75 yards. Loughlin converted Devine's try, a Lydon penalty pulling two points back for Wigan and leaving the interval score at 12-6 in St Helens favour.

Two offside decisions – both against Roy Haggarty – gave Lydon further kicking opportunities at the start of the second half, reducing St Helens' lead to two points.

Andy Goodway has the try-line in his sights for the match-winner following brilliant work by skipper Ellery Hanley (left).

It was Ged Byrne that put Wigan ahead on the hour, racing down the right flank to finish off a move instigated by Gregory. With the conversion attempt failing, it left Wigan hanging on to a 14-12 lead, the scores being tied ten minutes later when Loughlin landed his second penalty setting the stage for Hanley to produce his dramatic rescue act when a replay looked the most likely outcome.

Match statistics:
Wigan 20 St Helens 14
Rugby League Challenge Cup semi-final
Saturday 10 March 1990 at Old Trafford, Manchester (kick-off: 3.00 p.m.)

Wigan	*St Helens*
(blue and white irregular hoops)	(white with red V)

Full-back:
Steve Hampson (try)   Gary Connolly

Three-quarters:
Ged Byrne (try),   Alan Hunte, Phil Veivers,
Joe Lydon (4 goals),   Paul Loughlin (3 goals),
Kevin Iro, Mark Preston   Les Quirk (try)

Half-backs:
Shaun Edwards, Andy Gregory   Tommy Frodsham, Sean Devine (try)

Forwards:
Adrian Shelford, Martin Dermott,   Paul Forber, Paul Groves,
Andy Platt, Denis Betts,   George Mann, Bernard Dwyer,
Andy Goodway (try),   Roy Haggerty, Shane Cooper
Ellery Hanley (captain)   (captain)

Substitutes:
Bobbie Goulding for Gregory 31 min.   Andy Bateman for Cooper 53 min.
Ian Gildart for Betts 31 min.   Mark Bailey for Frodsham 60 min.
Gregory for Goulding 55 min.   Cooper for Forber 60 min.
Betts for Gildart 60 min.

Coach: *Coach:*
John Monie   Mike McClennan

Referee: Robin Whitfield (Widnes)   *Half-time:* 6-12
Attendance: 26,489   *Receipts:* £177,161
Weather: Cloudy, strong wind

First half:

10 min.	Hampson (Wigan)	try	4-0
21 min.	Loughlin (St Helens)	penalty	4-2
29 min.	Devine (St Helens)	try	4-6
	Loughlin (St Helens)	conversion	4-8
34 min.	Lydon (Wigan)	penalty	6-8
39 min.	Quirk (St Helens)	try	6-12

Second half:

43 min.	Lydon (Wigan)	penalty	8-12
53 min.	Lydon (Wigan)	penalty	10-12
60 min.	Byrne (Wigan)	try	14-12
70 min.	Loughlin (St Helens)	penalty	14-14
78 min.	Goodway (Wigan)	try	18-14
	Lydon (Wigan)	conversion	20-14

WIGAN v. WARRINGTON Rugby League Challenge Cup final
28 April 1990, Wembley Stadium, London

Wigan's third consecutive Wembley win put them into the record books and was every bit as convincing as the previous two. This time, their adversaries were Warrington, but like Halifax and St Helens before them, they struggled to come to terms with the power of Wigan's performance on the big stage.

Warrington showed some determined tackling in the early stages but, lacking regular goal-kicker Robert Turner, the job went to Paul Bishop, who missed two early penalty chances that could have settled Warrington nerves. Instead, it was Wigan's Joe Lydon who put over the first penalty, Bob Jackson being judged to have fouled Shaun Edwards after the stand-off had kicked the ball. With a quarter of the match gone, Dennis Betts touched down for the opening try (which was later converted by Lydon), pouncing on the ball after Edwards had charged down an attempted David Lyon clearance. Bishop finally put Warrington's first points on the board, a penalty in the 25th minute making it 8-2, but seven minutes later Wigan struck again. It came when Warrington centre Gary Mercer put in a short kick that landed in the arms of Mark Preston. The Wigan speed merchant shot away to register his side's second try. Lydon's conversion, plus a penalty five minutes later, put his side very much in the driving seat with a 16-2 lead. With half-time approaching, Bishop created a gap for his skipper Mike Gregory to grab Warrington's opening try, Bishop himself adding the extras.

Any thought of a comeback disappeared eight minutes into the second half, when Kevin Iro powered over after a telling break by Ellery Hanley. Six minutes later Preston got his second, finishing off a brilliant Wigan attacking move that covered the length of the field. Hanley scored Wigan's third try of the half after 63 minutes and, with Lydon converting two of them, it placed Wigan in an unassailable 32-8 lead. Lyon scored a consoling try for Warrington with five minutes to go, Paul Darbyshire converting. The scoring was completed in the final minutes when Iro claimed his sixth try in three Wembley appearances for Wigan.

In a match that again produced world record receipts, Wigan had defied the pain barrier, going into the game with Andy Gregory (whose guile earned his second Lance Todd Trophy), Hanley, Iro, Lydon and Andy Platt all less than 100 per cent.

Adrian Shelford about to pass to Bobbie Goulding. The supporting Wigan players are Denis Betts (at back) and Ellery Hanley (extreme right).

Edwards in particular went through the wars, with a broken hand (which received a pre-match painkiller) being added to by a 10th-minute facial injury that included a depressed cheekbone and fractured eye socket.

Match statistics:
Wigan 36 Warrington 14
Rugby League Challenge Cup final
Saturday 28 April 1990 at Wembley Stadium, London (kick-off: 3.00 p.m.)

Wigan	**Warrington**
(cherry and white irregular hoops)	(primrose and blue hoops)

Full-back:
Steve Hampson | David Lyon (try)

Three-quarters:
Joe Lydon (6 goals), Kevin Iro (2 tries), Dean Bell, Mark Preston (2 tries) | Des Drummond, Gary Mercer, Paul Darbyshire (goal), Mark Foster

Half-backs:
Shaun Edwards, Andy Gregory | Martin Crompton, Paul Bishop (2 goals)

Forwards:
Adrian Shelford, Martin Dermott, Andy Platt, Denis Betts (try), Andy Goodway, Ellery Hanley (captain, try) | Tony Burke, Duane Mann, Neil Harmon, Bob Jackson, Gary Sanderson, Mike Gregory (captain, try)

Substitutes:
Bobbie Goulding for Dermott 30 min.
Dermott for Goulding 63 min.
Ian Gildart for Preston 79 min.
Goulding for Edwards 79 min.
| Mark Thomas for Jackson 34 min.
Jackson for Burke 54 min.
Billy McGinty for Bishop 61 min.
Burke for Jackson 77 min.

Coach:
John Monie | *Coach:*
Brian Johnson

Referee: John Holdsworth (Kippax)
Attendance: 77,729
Weather: Sunny and warm
| *Half-time:* 16-8
Receipts: £1,360,000

First half:

12 min.	Lydon (Wigan)	penalty	2-0
21 min.	Betts (Wigan)	try	6-0
	Lydon (Wigan)	conversion	8-0
25 min.	Bishop (Warrington)	penalty	8-2
32 min.	Preston (Wigan)	try	12-2
	Lydon (Wigan)	conversion	14-2
37 min.	Lydon (Wigan)	penalty	16-2
40 min.	Gregory (Warrington)	try	16-6
	Bishop (Warrington)	conversion	16-8

Second half:

48 min.	Iro (Wigan)	try	20-8
	Lydon (Wigan)	conversion	22-8
54 min.	Preston (Wigan)	try	26-8
63 min.	Hanley (Wigan)	try	30-8
	Lydon (Wigan)	conversion	32-8
75 min.	Lyon (Warrington)	try	32-12
	Darbyshire (Warrington)	conversion	32-14
79 min.	Iro (Wigan)	try	36-14

WIGAN v. LEEDS Rugby League Championship
13 April 1991, Headingley, Leeds

Wigan retained their championship title at Headingley at the climax of what coach John Monie had called 'mission impossible'. They found themselves having to play the final eight League fixtures in a nineteen-day period. The first five were won, with fellow contenders Widnes coming to Central Park for a crucial 'four-pointer' in the sixth, drawing an attendance of 29,763. Wigan won 26-6 to go one point ahead of Widnes, the Cherry and Whites requiring one more victory to keep their crown. Two days later at Central Park, fatigue took its toll and they were held 18-18 by Bradford Northern. Everything depended on the last match at Leeds. Again, there was only a two-day gap and the question was would Wigan have anything left in the tank?

Bobbie Goulding, deputising for the injured Andy Gregory, played a massive part in the resultant triumph, scoring three precious drop goals. The first, after seven minutes, gave Wigan a slender but psychological lead that helped settle the nerves after a tentative start. Goulding also played a key role in the opening try after 25 minutes, providing an 'up-and-under' which had the Leeds defence in disarray as Andy Goodway caught the ball to touchdown. Frano Botica's conversion put Wigan a comforting two scores ahead at 7-0. Goulding claimed his second drop-kick before Simon Irving opened the home account with a penalty. A minute later, with half-time approaching, Ellery Hanley was the unlikely provider of another drop goal, making the interval score 9-2.

Any second-half anxiety was calmed with Goulding's third drop effort eight minutes after the restart, followed by a second try when Martin Dermott dived over from acting half-back, pushing Wigan 14-2 ahead. Garry Schofield killed off any complacency, putting John Bentley in for a try direct from a scrum, Irving's goal bringing Leeds back to within six points. To Wigan's relief, Botica was presented

Mission Complete!

Hanley's heroes defy the odds to clinch title in style

Leeds 8 Wigan 20

"You're by far the greatest team the world has ever seen!" The rapturous Cherry-and-White Army roared out their triumphant acclaim to John Monie's Marvels in the emotional scenes at Headingley on Saturday.

This was the unforgettable moment, as Ellery Hanley lifted aloft the Stones Bitter Championship Trophy for the third time in five fabulous years - and the record £44,000 winners' cheque to go with it. Never has it been more worthily deserved.

The trophy had been hidden under a binbag at Central Park two nights before Yet, the Invincibles kept the cherry-and-white ribbons on it in style

By John Benn

Mission Impossible completed. Wigan's wonderful walking-wounded stayed the course in the final gripping episode of the most punishing endurance test of all time — emerging victorious in their ninth big game in three weeks and their fifth within eight days.

An eighth League double meant that Widnes' hollow 44-20 win over doomed Rochdale Hornets on Sunday was meaningless

The Champs celebrate their title with a song. Pictures Peter Hill.

The match report from the *Wigan Observer* happily announces 'Mission (Impossible) Complete'.

with a penalty opportunity five minutes later that sailed between the posts. Denis Betts then signalled the terrace celebrations seven minutes from time, taking three defenders over the line as he touched down for the final score.

Chairman Maurice Lindsay, mindful of the gruelling run-in, proudly described the match as 'the greatest Championship triumph in the history of the game.' The effort did take its toll, however, a weary Wigan losing at home a week later to eighth-placed Featherstone Rovers in the opening round of the Premiership. This was followed by a 13-8 win over St Helens at Wembley in the least convincing of their eight consecutive Challenge Cup wins.

Match statistics:

Wigan 20 Leeds 8
Rugby League Championship
Saturday 13 April 1991 at Headingley, Leeds (kick-off: 2.45 p.m.)

Wigan	**Leeds**
(cherry and white irregular hoops)	(blue with amber bands)

Full-back:
Steve Hampson   John Gallagher

Three-quarters:
David Myers, Dean Bell, Andy   John Bentley (try), Carl Gibson,
Goodway (try), Frano Botica (2 goals)   Simon Irving (2 goals), Phil Ford

Half-backs:
Shaun Edwards   Garry Schofield (captain)
Bobbie Goulding (3 drop goals)   Paul Harkin

Forwards:
Ian Lucas, Martin Dermott (try),   Roy Powell, Colin Maskill,
Andy Platt, Denis Betts (try), Phil   Shaun Wane, Cavill Heugh,
Clarke, Ellery Hanley (captain, drop goal) Paul Dixon, David Heron

Substitutes:
Ian Gildart for Hanley 51 min.   Gary Divorty for Heugh 48 min.
Kevin Iro (did not play)   Gary Lord for Gibson 72 min.

Coach: *Coach:*
John Monie   David Ward

Referee: John Holdsworth (Kippax)   *Half-time:* 9-2
Attendance: 15,313   *Weather:* Overcast

First half:

7 min.	Goulding (Wigan)	drop goal	1-0
25 min.	Goodway (Wigan)	try	5-0
	Botica (Wigan)	conversion	7-0
30 min.	Goulding (Wigan)	drop goal	8-0
38 min.	Irving (Leeds)	penalty	8-2
39 min.	Hanley (Wigan)	drop goal	9-2

Second half:

48 min.	Goulding (Wigan)	drop goal	10-2
55 min.	Dermott (Wigan)	try	14-2
62 min.	Bentley (Leeds)	try	14-6
	Irving (Leeds)	conversion	14-8
67 min.	Botica (Wigan)	penalty	16-8
73 min.	Betts (Wigan)	try	20-8

WIGAN v. PENRITH PANTHERS World Club Challenge
2 October 1991, Anfield, Liverpool

Wigan again reached the heights in club football by recapturing the world crown after a four-year gap. Opponents Penrith Panthers travelled to England with a big reputation following a superb season in Australia, climaxed by their 19-12 Grand Final victory over Canberra Raiders just ten days earlier. It was Wigan, however, who demonstrated greater commitment and determination under the Anfield floodlights of Liverpool AFC.

The British champions had to overcome the pre-match blow of losing centre Dean Bell, who broke down in the onfield warm-up before the game and, unselfishly, declared himself unfit. His place went to Sam Panapa, originally scheduled for a wing spot, David Myers taking over on the flank. It was a cruel blow for Bell, who had also withdrawn from the 1987 clash with Manly-Warringah through injury.

Penrith began the match in a vigorous manner, dishing out what could politely be described as some 'big hits', including a late tackle by Steve Carter on Andy Gregory. French referee Alain Sablayrolles repeatedly penalised the Australians, the ever-reliable boot of Frano Botica making them pay the price. He landed four goals in the first 13 minutes – the third from the halfway line after the Panthers scrum-half and skipper Greg Alexander had kicked the ball directly out of play when restarting the game – opening up an 8-0 lead. Botica's performance of landing six vital goals from seven attempts and a try-saving tackle on the outstanding Penrith second-row man John Cartwright earned him the 'Man of the Match' award.

Penrith, who never led at any stage, scored the first try of the night – and their only points all evening – when winger Darren Willis followed up a neat kick-through from Greg Alexander. Nine minutes later Gregory responded by putting Panapa in for Wigan's opening touchdown, Botica's goal settling the half-time score at 14-4.

Another world title! Left to right, standing: Dennis Wright (physiotherapist), Sam Panapa, David Myers, Ian Lucas, Shaun Edwards, Billy McGinty, Mike Forshaw, Neil Cowie, Kelvin Skerrett, Ian Gildart, Denis Betts, Andy Platt, Phil Clarke. Kneeling: Billy Shaw (kit-man), Frano Botica, Martin Dermott, John Monie (coach, with trophy), Joe Lydon, Andy Gregory (captain), Steve Hampson. Also pictured are time-keeper Keith Hayton (behind Edwards' outstretched arm) and physiotherapist Keith Mills (behind Platt).

WIGAN v. PENRITH PANTHERS

Wigan, who had lost influential prop Kelvin Skerrett after 37 minutes due to an ankle injury, defended resolutely in the second half as Penrith, exerting greater pressure aided by better ball-retention, were held close to the line several times. The Wigan defence held out, Botica giving his colleagues massive encouragement with his fifth penalty ten minutes from full time. In the dying minutes, Wigan confirmed their success when Shaun Edwards raced over half the length of the field after intercepting a pass to send Myers over, Joe Lydon dropping a goal in the final seconds. After the match, shirts were quickly exchanged, providing the unique sight of all seventeen Wigan players sporting Penrith colours for the cup presentation.

Match statistics:
Wigan 21 Penrith Panthers 4
World Club Challenge
Wednesday 2 October 1991 at Anfield, Liverpool (kick-off: 8.00 p.m.)

Wigan	**Penrith Panthers**
(cherry and white hoops)	(black and white)

Full-back:
Steve Hampson	Greg Barwick

Three-quarters:
David Myers (try), Sam Panapa (try),	Darren Willis (try), Graeme Bradley,
Joe Lydon (drop goal), Frano Botica (6 goals)	Brad Izzard, Graham Mackay

Half-backs:
Shaun Edwards, Andy Gregory (captain)	Steve Carter, Greg Alexander (captain)

Forwards:
Kelvin Skerrett, Martin Dermott,	Brandon Lee, Royce Simmons,
Andy Platt, Denis Betts,	Paul Dunn, Paul Clarke,
Billy McGinty, Phil Clarke	John Cartwright, Colin van der Voort

Substitutes:
Neil Cowie for Skerrett 37 min.	Ben Alexander for Barwick 40 min.
Ian Gildart for McGinty 65 min.	Grant Izzard for Lee 40 min.
Ian Lucas for Cowie 75 min.	Paul Smith for Willis 50 min.
Mike Forshaw for Clarke 75 min.	Tony Xuereb for van der Voort 60 min.

Coach:
John Monie	*Coach:* Phil Gould

Referee: Alain Sablayrolles (France)
Attendance: 20,152
Weather: Cloudy, dry conditions

Half-time: 14-4
Receipts: £179,797

First half:

4 min.	Botica (Wigan)	penalty	2-0
8 min.	Botica (Wigan)	penalty	4-0
10 min.	Botica (Wigan)	penalty	6-0
13 min.	Botica (Wigan)	penalty	8-0
18 min.	Willis (Penrith Panthers)	try	8-4
27 min.	Panapa (Wigan)	try	12-4
	Botica (Wigan)	conversion	14-4

Second half:

70 min.	Botica (Wigan)	penalty	16-4
77 min.	Myers (Wigan)	try	20-4
80 min.	Lydon (Wigan)	drop goal	21-4

WIGAN v. BRADFORD NORTHERN Rugby League Challenge Cup
semi-final, 28 March 1992, Burnden Park, Bolton

Many critics believe the Wigan team of this era was at its most awesome during the 1991/92 season, the breathtaking Challenge Cup semi-final performance against Bradford Northern providing ample proof for that argument. Wigan's relentless pressure throughout was described by Alex Murphy as 'one of the greatest team performances for a long, long time.' The team was certainly reaching new height, a fact all the more remarkable when it is realised the influential Ellery Hanley had joined Leeds six months earlier.

Andy Gregory demonstrated Wigan's commitment to victory during the first raid into Northern territory, with a neat drop goal in the third minute. Gregory also initiated the moves leading to the opening tries from forwards Denis Betts and Ian Lucas, both goaled by Frano Botica, for a 13-0 lead after 16 minutes. Four minutes later, Northern, for the only time in the opening half, threatened when David Hobbs kicked into the corner, Joe Lydon just beating Gerald Cordle to the touchdown. Despite the score, Bradford had tackled well but in the final 20 minutes of the half their big pack could not cope with the speed of Wigan's attacking machine. Four more tries came before the interval; from Gene Miles (after a wonderful Lydon break from inside his own 25), Martin Offiah, Joe Lydon (after a length-of-the-field run from Dean Bell) and Shaun Edwards (from a Gregory up-and-under). Botica hit the post following Offiah's score, but converted the others for a staggering 35-0 half-time lead.

Despite the damp Burnden Park pitch cutting up, the second-half pressure on Bradford was unrelenting. Offiah scored his second try within three minutes and added three more to finish with five on the day. His last, in the dying minutes, was the best solo effort of the game, receiving the ball on his own 25 and flying down the touchline past three defenders to finish under the posts. Others came from Bell (another great attacking move which began in Wigan's 25 as the ball went through five pairs of hands in bewildering fashion), Botica and Miles. Northern had scant consolation, with tries from Darrall Shelford and Henderson Gill, the latter receiving a warm round of applause from the Wigan contingent for their former hero.

The final 71-10 score was easily a record for a Challenge Cup semi-final, although Northern could claim they were missing several players through injury. Man of the Match Miles had a massive impact during his one season at Central Park, Offiah later saying the Aussie was one of the best centre-partners he ever had.

FRANO BOTICA

WIGAN

On the mark. Frano Botica with nine goals for Wigan.

Match statistics:
Wigan 71 Bradford Northern 10
Rugby League Challenge Cup semi-final
Saturday 28 March 1992 at Burnden Park, Bolton (kick-off: 3.00 p.m.)

Wigan	*Bradford Northern*
(cherry and white irregular hoops)	(white with red, amber and black V)

Full-back:
Joe Lydon (try)   Alex Green

Three-quarters:
Frano Botica (try, 9 goals)   Gerald Cordle
Dean Bell (captain, try)   Darrall Shelford (try)
Gene Miles (2 tries)   Roger Simpson
Martin Offiah (5 tries)   Henderson Gill (try)

Half-backs:
Shaun Edwards (try)   Neil Summers
Andy Gregory (drop goal)   Brett Iti

Forwards:
Ian Lucas (try), Martin Dermott,   Paul Grayshon, Brian Noble,
Andy Platt, Denis Betts (try),   Jon Hamer, Paul Medley, David
Bill McGinty, Phil Clarke   Hobbs (captain, goal), Karl Fairbank

Substitutes:
Neil Cowie for McGinty 28 min.   Craig Richards for Grayshon 28 min.
Kelvin Skerrett for Lucas 28 min.   David Croft for Hamer 40 min.
Lucas for Betts 40 min.   Hamer for Iti 53 min.
McGinty for Platt 70 min.   Grayshon for Richards 59 min.

Blood-bin replacement:

Richards for Hamer 18-25 min.

Coach: *Coach:*
John Monie   Peter Fox

Referee: Robin Whitfield (Widnes)   *Half-time:* 35-0
Attendance: 18,027   *Receipts:* £131,124
Weather: Overcast and mild, damp

First half:

3 min.	Gregory (Wigan)	drop goal	1-0
12 min.	Betts/Botica (Wigan)	try/conversion	7-0
16 min.	Lucas/Botica (Wigan)	try/conversion	13-0
23 min.	Miles/Botica (Wigan)	try/conversion	19-0
35 min.	Offiah (Wigan)	try	23-0
38 min.	Lydon/Botica (Wigan)	try/conversion	29-0
40 min.	Edwards/Botica (Wigan)	try/conversion	35-0

Second half:

43 min.	Offiah (Wigan)	try	39-0
46 min.	Shelford (Bradford N)	try	39-4
52 min.	Offiah/Botica (Wigan)	try/conversion	45-4
55 min.	Bell (Wigan)	try	49-4
66 min.	Offiah (Wigan)	try	53-4
70 min.	Gill/Hobbs (Bradford N)	try/conversion	53-10
74 min.	Botica/Botica (Wigan)	try/conversion	59-10
76 min.	Miles/Botica (Wigan)	try/conversion	65-10
78 min.	Offiah/Botica (Wigan)	try/conversion	71-10

WIGAN v. LEEDS Premiership Trophy semi-final
10 May 1992, Central Park, Wigan

Sometimes there are moments in sport so unexpected and out of the ordinary they cannot be explained and those present return home trying to rationalise what they have witnessed. The Wigan contingent among the 18,000-plus spectators who streamed out of Central Park that Sunday afternoon in May 1992 may well have been delighted that their team had reached their first Premiership Trophy final in five years, but the real talk of the town was Martin Offiah's ten tries. If it had been an opening round Challenge Cup tie against an amateur side (no disrespect to amateur clubs intended!) then maybe, just maybe, it would have been feasible, but supporters were left asking themselves 'Did Offiah really score ten tries against top opposition like Leeds in a major competition semi-final?' The final tally of 74-6 represented a record for the Premiership and the biggest score Leeds had conceded in any competitive match.

Offiah scored five in each half between the 7th and 67th minutes of the game – in other words, in just one hour's play! After Offiah's first, it appeared that it would be team captain Dean Bell who would be in line for a hat-trick as he ran in the next two, including a wonderful 60-yard run. The remaining four tries of the half all belonged to Offiah, who later said: 'I didn't realise until (club physio) Keith Mills told me at half-time that I was within two of equalling the Wigan club record.'

Two minutes after the restart, it was hooker Martin Dermott who notched the next Wigan try, before Offiah resumed his torment of Leeds and their coach Doug Laughton (who had, ironically, introduced him to Rugby League with Widnes from Rosslyn Park RU in 1987), racing in for the next five tries. The second of those – in

Martin Offiah is cheered on as he heads for the try-line once more, having been put clear by Dean Bell (right).

Well done Martin! Skipper Dean Bell (right) acknowledges another try by the flying winger.

Two Leeds defenders are stranded as 'Chariots' Offiah dives over in the corner for yet another touchdown!

WIGAN v. LEEDS

Shaun Edwards (left) helps Martin Offiah to indicate his final try tally. It was a prophetic gesture, with Edwards equalling the record four months later!

the 56th minute – tied the Wigan record of seven, held jointly by Johnny Ring, Gordon Ratcliffe, Billy Boston and Green Vigo. It was in the build-up to that try that former Wigan player Bobbie Goulding flattened Shaun Edwards, resulting in the Leeds half-back's permanent dismissal from the game while Edwards, with a badly gashed eye, later visited the local hospital for an X-ray. With centres Gene Miles and Bell laying on chance after chance for Offiah, who was popping up all over the field, he reached his tenth with 13 minutes of the game remaining. David Myers scored the remaining Wigan try, Paul Dixon getting a late try for Leeds.

As a footnote, Shaun Edwards equalled Offiah's record the following September against second division Swinton in a Lancashire Cup tie.

Match statistics:
Wigan 74 Leeds 6
Premiership Trophy semi-final
Sunday 10 May 1992 at Central Park, Wigan (kick-off: 3.00 p.m.)

Wigan	**Leeds**
(cherry and white irregular hoops)	(blue and amber)

Full-back:
Steve Hampson — Phil Ford

Three-quarters:

Joe Lydon	Leigh Deakin
Dean Bell (captain, 2 tries)	Morvin Edwards
Gene Miles	Carl Gibson
Martin Offiah (10 tries)	Vince Fawcett

Half-backs:

Frano Botica (9 goals)	Craig Innes
Shaun Edwards	Bobbie Goulding

Forwards:

Neil Cowie	Steve Molloy
Martin Dermott (try)	Colin Maskill (goal)
Andy Platt	Shaun Wane
Denis Betts	Gary Divorty
Billy McGinty	Paul Dixon (try)
Phil Clarke	Garry Schofield (captain)

Substitutes:

Sam Panapa for McGinty 27 min.	John Bentley for Deakin 27 min.
David Myers (try) for Lydon 46 min.	Stuart Arundel for Schofield 49 min.
McGinty for Dermott 49 min.	

Blood-bin replacement:
Lydon for Edwards 58 min.

Coach:	*Coach:*
John Monie	Doug Laughton

Referee: Colin Morris (Huddersfield)   *Half-time:* 36-0
Attendance: 18,261   *Weather:* Sunny and warm

First half:

7 min.	Offiah (Wigan)	try	4-0
15 min.	Bell (Wigan)	try	8-0
17 min.	Bell/Botica (Wigan)	try/conversion	14-0
23 min.	Offiah/Botica (Wigan)	try/conversion	20-0
27 min.	Offiah/Botica (Wigan)	try/conversion	26-0
35 min.	Offiah (Wigan)	try	30-0
40 min.	Offiah/Botica (Wigan)	try/conversion	36-0

Second half:

42 min.	Dermott (Wigan)	try	40-0
45 min.	Offiah (Wigan)	try	44-0
56 min.	Offiah/Botica (Wigan)	try/conversion	50-0
60 min.	Offiah/Botica (Wigan)	try/conversion	56-0
63 min.	Offiah/Botica (Wigan)	try/conversion	62-0
67 min.	Offiah/Botica (Wigan)	try/conversion	68-0
73 min.	Myers/Botica (Wigan)	try/conversion	74-0
80 min.	Dixon/Maskill (Leeds)	try/conversion	74-6

WIGAN v. ST HELENS Premiership Trophy final
17 May 1992, Old Trafford, Manchester

In the baking heat of a hot Sunday afternoon at Old Trafford, Wigan followed their record-making Premiership semi-final win over Leeds with another milestone performance in the final against St Helens. It is difficult to imagine where Wigan got their reserves of energy from to score six tries in the final half hour – creating a record score for a Rugby League final in any competition in the process – when it is realised that the Saints led 12-10 until the 52nd minute. The win completed a unique treble, adding to the League title and Challenge Cup victories that season, as Wigan notched their 26th consecutive victory. The match – despite a reduced capacity due to rebuilding work at the Stretford End of the ground – produced record receipts for the competition from a 'sell out' attendance.

St Helens started the stronger but, after an early exchange of penalties which made the score 2-2, Saints' skipper Shane Cooper was sin-binned in the 18th minute after kicking out at Shaun Edwards. Frano Botica kicked the resultant penalty and, with St Helens reduced temporarily to twelve men, Andy Platt was able to 'dummy' his way over the try-line five minutes later, Botica's conversion making the score 10-2. St Helens, still down to twelve men, recovered when Paul Bishop and George Mann sent Paul Loughlin on his way, scoring a try in the corner. Loughlin raised the morale of the Saints' fans when he added the extra two points with an excellent touchline kick. Before half-time St Helens took a 12-10 lead when Anthony Sullivan outpaced Edwards in a 30-yard dash for the try-line.

After the interval, St Helens were looking to increase their lead and were deep in opposition territory when Wigan scored a glorious try which changed the momentum of the game. Edwards – who was playing at scrum-half for the injured Andy Gregory – set up Australian centre Gene Miles for a powerful run downfield. His perfectly timed pass to Martin Offiah sent the flying winger on a thrilling 45-yard run to score under the posts, this despite the fact Offiah was not fully fit. With St Helens wilting in the heat, Wigan sensed their moment and gave the ball plenty of air. The try count mounted quickly as Denis Betts (two), David Myers, Miles (in his final game for Wigan) and Offiah (with his second) went over, Botica punishing Saints by converting every one and adding a penalty for a 48-12 lead, Sullivan grabbing a late consolation try for the runners-up.

Wigan just different class

| St Helens | 16 |
| Wigan | 48 |

Raymond Fletcher

ALL-CONQUERING Wigan surpassed even their greatest moments in a remarkable season with a seven-try demolition of St Helens that almost defied description.

Their 48 points were not only a record for the Stones Bitter Premiership final but the most scored in any final during the game's near 100-year history — as were Frano Botica's 10 goals.

It was oh so inspiring. The 7-10 Challenge Cup semi-final thrashing of Bradford Northern and last week's 74-6 caning of Leeds were mere training runs compared with this.

St Helens are Britain's second best team and were expected to give Wigan a tough game. For just over 50 minutes they did and deservedly led 12-10.

After 21 successive wins Wigan looked ready to be taken as the sun scorched down and the obvious assumption was that they were burnt out.

Then Wigan found not so much a second win as a hurricane force that blew away the opposition. It struck with devastating suddenness and brought six tries in 25 stunning minutes.

There was a blinding flash of black action from Martin Offiah to herald Wigan's glorious finale. After his 10-try humiliation of Leeds,

the pressure was on for Offiah to produce something special again and he struggled to get into the game until given his first real opportunity.

Then Gene Miles powered down the middle before sending his winger high-stepping out of a tackle and galumphing 40 yards to the posts.

It was what everybody except St Helens fans had come to see and there was more to follow. Wigan had raced to a 36-12 lead when Offiah appeared from nowhere to get through clutching hands for a try behind the posts.

Thirty tries in 16 matches or 25 in nine, however the figures are presented they can only indicate that Offiah is a modern phenomenal.

Botica's goalkicking also produced some interesting statistics as he followed up his five out five at Wembley with more 100 per cent success from 10 attempts and his 20 points were another Premiership final record.

Although Shaun Edwards did not add to his leadership total of 40 tries he was a key figure in Wigan's late onslaught which brought tries from Denis Betts (two), David Myers and Miles.

St Helens were devastated but Anthony Sullivan at least had the satisfaction of adding a second try in the last minute. His first had given St Helens a surprise 12-10 lead seven minute before the interval.

Paul Loughlin had created the chance after the centre had broken away for St Helens's first try a few minutes earlier and added his second goal.

Wigan had taken a 10-2 lead inside 22 minutes with three Botica goals and a smart try from Andy Platt, who dummied his way through from close range.

The try, added to his usual high workrate, helped the prop to the Harry Sunderland Trophy as man-of-the-match for which there were many contenders.

My vote went to Martin Dermott, Wigan's hooker who lost the scrums 8-2 but looked as lively as any half-back.

The *Yorkshire Post*'s Raymond Fletcher was clearly impressed by a Wigan performance 'that almost defied description.'

Match statistics:
Wigan 48 St Helens 16
Premiership Trophy final
Sunday 17 May 1992 at Old Trafford, Manchester (kick-off: 3.30 p.m.)

Wigan	**St Helens**
(cherry and white irregular hoops)	(blue and white)

Full-back:
Steve Hampson — Phil Veivers

Three-quarters:
Joe Lydon, Dean Bell (captain), Gene Miles (try), Martin Offiah (2 tries) — Alan Hunte, Gary Connolly, Paul Loughlin (try, 2 goals), Anthony Sullivan (2 tries)

Half-backs:
Frano Botica (10 goals), Shaun Edwards — Tea Ropati, Paul Bishop

Forwards:
Neil Cowie, Martin Dermott, Andy Platt (try), Denis Betts (2 tries), Billy McGinty, Phil Clarke — Jonathan Neil, Bernard Dwyer, Kevin Ward, Sonny Nickle, George Mann, Shane Cooper (captain)

Substitutes:
Sam Panapa for McGinty 28 min.
David Myers (try) for Hampson 62 min.

Jonathan Griffiths for Connolly 40 min.
Paul Groves for Neil 55 min.

Coach:
John Monie

Coach:
Mike McClennan

Referee: John Holdsworth (Kippax)
Attendance: 33,157
Weather: Sunny and hot

Half-time: 10-12
Receipts: £389,988

First half:

Time	Scorer	Type	Score
5 min.	Loughlin (St Helens)	penalty	0-2
10 min.	Botica (Wigan)	penalty	2-2
18 min.	Botica (Wigan)	penalty	4-2
23 min.	Platt (Wigan)	try	8-2
	Botica (Wigan)	conversion	10-2
27 min.	Loughlin (St Helens)	try	10-6
	Loughlin (St Helens)	conversion	10-8
33 min.	Sullivan (St Helens)	try	10-12

Second half:

Time	Scorer	Type	Score
52 min.	Offiah (Wigan)	try	14-12
	Botica (Wigan)	conversion	16-12
58 min.	Botica (Wigan)	penalty	18-12
59 min.	Betts (Wigan)	try	22-12
	Botica (Wigan)	conversion	24-12
64 min.	Myers (Wigan)	try	28-12
	Botica (Wigan)	conversion	30-12
69 min.	Miles (Wigan)	try	34-12
	Botica (Wigan)	conversion	36-12
73 min.	Offiah (Wigan)	try	40-12
	Botica (Wigan)	conversion	42-12
77 min.	Betts (Wigan)	try	46-12
	Botica (Wigan)	conversion	48-12
79 min.	Sullivan (St Helens)	try	48-16

WIGAN v. ST HELENS Lancashire Challenge Cup final
18 October 1992, Knowsley Road, St Helens

This tryless Lancashire Cup final between Wigan and St Helens was to make history, although the full extent of it was not fully appreciated at the time. The reclaiming of the trophy after a four-year gap completed the 'set' for Wigan coach John Monie, being the only one to have evaded him during his tenure at Central Park. More poignantly, it was the last time the famous old trophy was competed for, the decision being taken (later) that the competition, along with the Yorkshire Cup, was too parochial and no longer fitted the modern image the sport was striving for. Wigan, who won the first contest in 1905, left their mark with 21 wins from 35 final appearances, both of which were easily competition records.

With no suitable neutral venue available to stage the final, the two clubs tossed a coin for 'home' advantage, St Helens winning. This was the second time they had faced this dilemma, Wigan staging the 1984 County final between the two adversaries. It was a move that paid off, literally, as the receipts generated set a new record for both the Lancashire Cup and the Knowsley Road ground, the turnstiles being closed 25 minutes before the start, leaving thousands locked out.

Although the match was decided without anyone crossing the 'whitewash' for a touchdown it was, nonetheless, an exciting final, fiercely contested by both packs with the props on both sides making an outstanding contribution in a tough, hard-fought, encounter. For Great Britain coach Malcolm Reilly, watching from the stand, it was a nervous experience, coming six days before Great Britain – who had eleven players involved in the match – met Australia in the World Cup final at Wembley.

The Wigan team relish what was to be their final Lancashire Cup success. From left to right, standing: Andy Platt, Shaun Edwards, Billy McGinty, Neil Cowie, Kelvin Skerrett, Denis Betts, Martin Crompton, Steve Hampson, Andrew Farrar, Martin Offiah. Kneeling: Frano Botica, John Monie (coach), Dean Bell (captain), Martin Dermott, Joe Lydon, Jason Robinson, Chris Butler (conditioner).

As indicated from a scoreboard containing just five goals, defences were well on top throughout, Wigan taking the early initiative by recording all their points in the first-half through the trusty boot of former All Black Frano Botica. After 12 minutes he opened the scoring with a 30-yard drop goal, giving the scoreboard an unlikely display of 1-0 until the 23rd minute, when he kicked the first of his two penalties, the second being added nine minutes later.

After the break, St Helens clawed their way back with two penalty goals from hooker Bernard Dwyer. The second, with 12 minutes remaining, brought an expected onslaught from the Saints as they searched for a winner or at least an equalizing drop goal to force a replay. Thankfully for Wigan, their well-drilled defence saw them through to the final hooter and the £9,000 prize.

Match statistics:

Wigan 5 St Helens 4
Lancashire Challenge Cup final
Sunday 18 October 1992 at Knowsley Road, St Helens (kick-off: 3.00 p.m.)

Wigan	**St Helens**
(blue and white hoops)	(red and white)

Full-back:
Steve Hampson — Phil Veivers

Three-quarters:
Jason Robinson, Joe Lydon, Andrew Farrar, Martin Offiah — Alan Hunte, Gary Connolly, Jarrod McCracken, Anthony Sullivan

Half-backs:
Frano Botica (2 goals, drop goal), Shaun Edwards — Tea Ropati, Jonathan Griffiths

Forwards:
Kelvin Skerrett, Martin Dermott, Andy Platt, Denis Betts, Billy McGinty, Dean Bell (captain) — John Harrison, Bernard Dwyer (2 goals), Kevin Ward, Chris Joynt, Sonny Nickle, Shane Cooper (captain)

Substitutes:
Neil Cowie for Hampson 24 min.
Martin Crompton for Offiah 40 min.
Offiah for Crompton 65 min.

Gus O'Donnell for Connolly 29 min.
Connolly for O'Donnell 40 min.
O'Donnell for Veivers 51 min.
Paul Forber for Harrison 65 min.

Coach:
John Monie

Coach:
Mike McClennan

Referee: Stuart Cummings (Widnes)
Attendance: 20,534
Weather: Showery rain, cool

Half-time: 5-0
Receipts: £122,327

First half:

12 min.	Botica (Wigan)	drop goal	1-0
23 min.	Botica (Wigan)	penalty	3-0
32 min.	Botica (Wigan)	penalty	5-0

Second half:

45 min.	Dwyer (St Helens)	penalty	5-2
68 min.	Dwyer (St Helens)	penalty	5-4

WIGAN v. WIDNES Rugby League Challenge Cup final
1 May 1993, Wembley Stadium, London

Wigan began the 1993 Challenge Cup final as 5 to 1-on favourites and, although they justified that confidence with a sixth consecutive triumph, Widnes provided their toughest Wembley test for years in a very competitive match. It was the second Wembley final to see a player receive his marching orders (following Leeds' Syd Hynes in 1971) when Richard Eyres was ordered off after 65 minutes for aiming an elbow at the head of former Widnes colleague Martin Offiah. Many felt it could have even been a double sending off for Widnes when Bobbie Goulding escaped with a warning from referee Russell Smith following a high tackle on Jason Robinson four minutes from time.

It was Eyres that opened the afternoon's scoring after seven minutes, Goulding having prised open the Wigan defence. Jonathan Davies added the goal to place the Chemics 6-0 up. It was a short-lived lead, Kelvin Skerrett charging over for Wigan four minutes later, brushing aside two defenders in the process, Frano Botica's goal levelling the scores. Anyone who expected Wigan to open the floodgates at this point and justify why they were the bookies favourite was in for a surprise. Instead, it was Widnes' New Zealand prop Kurt Sorenson that went on a rampaging run from 25 yards out to score the next try after 17 minutes, bringing Wembley alight as the crowd began to anticipate an upset. Davies tagged on the extras to restore their six-point advantage. Again, Widnes failed to hold on, literally, as their winger John Devereux spilled the ball, Offiah seizing it to send Dean Bell in for a simple touchdown. Botica's conversion took him past Fred Griffiths' 1958/59 club record of 176 for a season. He then added a penalty on half-time, when Andy Currier strayed offside, putting Wigan in front for the first time with a 14-12 interval lead.

The second half proved just as tight, the only try going the way of Wigan two minutes after the restart, Bell putting substitute Sam Panapa through. Botica's goal provided Wigan's final points, a Davies penalty being the only remaining score.

Phil Clarke spots a gap in the Widnes defence as Steve Hampson (in skull-cap) races up in support.

The switching of skipper Bell (who took the Lance Todd Trophy) from his starting role at loose-forward to his customary centre spot after 30 minutes provided Wigan with better balance. It enabled Phil Clarke to take over at loose-forward where he, along with second row Denis Betts, had an influential match. Andy Farrell, who replaced Skerrett in the 55th minute, became Wembley's youngest winner a month short of his eighteenth birthday.

Match statistics:
Wigan 20 Widnes 14
Rugby League Challenge Cup final
Saturday 1 May 1993 at Wembley Stadium, London (kick-off: 2.30 p.m.)

Wigan	**Widnes**
(cherry and white hoops)	(white with black and red V's)

Full-back:
Steve Hampson — Stuart Spruce

Three-quarters:
Jason Robinson, Joe Lydon, Andrew Farrar, Martin Offiah — John Devereux, Andy Currier, Darren Wright, David Myers

Half-backs:
Frano Botica (4 goals), Shaun Edwards — Jonathan Davies (3 goals), Bobbie Goulding

Forwards:
Kelvin Skerrett (try), Martin Dermott, Andy Platt, Denis Betts, Phil Clarke, Dean Bell (captain, try) — Kurt Sorensen (try), Paul Hulme (captain), Harvey Howard, Richard Eyres (try), Esene Faimalo, David Hulme

Substitutes:
Sam Panapa (try) for Lydon 30 min.
Andy Farrell for Skerrett 55 min.
Skerrett for Platt 72 mins.
Lydon for Offiah 79 min.

Julian O'Neill for Faimalo 28 min.
Faimalo for Sorensen 40 min.
Steve McCurrie for Currier 55 min.
Currier for Wright 72 min.

Coach:
John Monie

Coach:
Phil Larder

Referee: Russell Smith (Castleford)
Attendance: 77,684
Weather: Sunny, very warm

Half-time: 14-12
Receipts: £1,981,591

First half:

Time	Player	Type	Score
7 min.	Eyres (Widnes)	try	0-4
	Davies (Widnes)	conversion	0-6
11 min.	Skerrett (Wigan)	try	4-6
	Botica (Wigan)	conversion	6-6
17 min.	Sorensen (Widnes)	try	6-10
	Davies (Widnes)	conversion	6-12
23 min.	Bell (Wigan)	try	10-12
	Botica (Wigan)	conversion	12-12
40 min.	Botica (Wigan)	penalty	14-12

Second half:

Time	Player	Type	Score
42 min.	Panapa (Wigan)	try	18-12
	Botica (Wigan)	conversion	20-12
49 min.	Davies (Widnes)	penalty	20-14

WIGAN v. LEEDS Rugby League Challenge Cup final
30 April 1994, Wembley Stadium, London

Martin Offiah won the Lance Todd Trophy for a second time after scoring two crucial tries against Leeds in the 1994 Wembley showpiece. Both efforts were spectacular, but the first, after 13 minutes play, has to be rated as the best ever at the historic stadium. Receiving a pass in front of his own posts, Offiah accelerated through a gap to go screaming down the right touchline, finally outmanoeuvring Leeds full-back Alan Tait on the outside for a memorable try in the corner.

Offiah's try had come just two minutes after Leeds had almost opened the scoring themselves, Garry Schofield being prevented from placing the ball after crossing the Wigan line. Leeds succumbed again in the 26th minute when a high ball from the boot of Shaun Edwards was not held by Tait, bouncing off his chest into the waiting arms of Andy Farrell, who touched down. Frano Botica added the goal to put Wigan ten points up. Although Leeds, ably led by former Wigan hero Ellery Hanley, made inroads into Wigan territory, it was a Botica penalty that completed the first-half scoring, the Cherry and Whites leading 12-0 at that stage.

Leeds looked as though they meant business when the second period began, Graham Holroyd getting their first points via a penalty two minutes into the half. This seemed to lift the Yorkshire side, hitting Wigan with two tries in a six-minute spell. The first was set up through an up-and-under from Schofield which Wigan full-back Gary Connolly failed to grasp, Leeds hooker James Lowes picking up the loose ball to feed winger Jim Fallon, who powered over. The second again involved Fallon, who recovered a loose ball lost by Barrie-Jon Mather in a tackle to set up Schofield, who sidestepped Offiah to score. Although Holroyd missed both conversions, Leeds, now only two points in arrears, appeared to have grabbed the momentum in the wilting afternoon heat. It was Offiah, with another stunning try in the 62nd minute, who regained the initiative for Wigan. It was set up by Mick Cassidy who, having beaten the Leeds cover, sent him racing in from the halfway line. Botica's conversion plus a penalty four minutes before Offiah's effort put Wigan 20-10 in front. Only eleven minutes from time Sam Panapa scored another,

Martin Offiah on the way to scoring one of Wembley's greatest ever solo tries in the 13th minute, having taken Leeds full-back Alan Tait (right) on the outside.

Botica again adding the goal. Leeds had the last word when Francis Cummins, at 17 years and 200 days the youngest player to appear at Wembley, covered over 80 yards to score a try after recovering Offiah's dropped pass. Holroyd's goal completed the scoring at 26-16 for Wigan.

Match statistics:
Wigan 26 Leeds 16
Rugby League Challenge Cup final
Saturday 30 April 1994 at Wembley Stadium, London (kick-off: 2.30 p.m.)

Wigan	**Leeds**
(cherry and white hoops)	(blue with amber band)

Full-back:
Gary Connolly — Alan Tait

Three-quarters:
Va'aiga Tuigamala, Dean Bell (captain), Barrie-Jon Mather, Martin Offiah (2 tries) — Jim Fallon (try), Kevin Iro, Craig Innes, Francis Cummins (try)

Half-backs:
Frano Botica (5 goals) — Graham Holroyd (2 goals)
Shaun Edwards — Garry Schofield (try)

Forwards:
Kelvin Skerrett, Martin Dermott, Andy Platt, Denis Betts, Andy Farrell (try), Phil Clarke — Neil Harmon, James Lowes, Harvey Howard, Gary Mercer, Richard Eyres, Ellery Hanley (captain)

Substitutes:
Mick Cassidy for Farrell 52 min. — Mike O'Neill for Harmon 65 min.
Sam Panapa (try) for Platt 62 min. — Marcus Vassilakopoulos for Hanley 73 min.
Platt for Dermott 72 min.
Farrell for Betts 78 min.

Coach:
John Dorahy

Coach:
Doug Laughton

Referee: David Campbell (Widnes)
Attendance: 78,348
Weather: Sunny, very hot

Half-time: 12-0
Receipts: £2,032,839

First half:

13 min.	Offiah (Wigan)	try	4-0
26 min.	Farrell (Wigan)	try	8-0
	Botica (Wigan)	conversion	10-0
36 min.	Botica (Wigan)	penalty	12-0

Second half:

42 min.	Holroyd (Leeds)	penalty	12-2
46 min.	Fallon (Leeds)	try	12-6
51 min.	Schofield (Leeds)	try	12-10
58 min.	Botica (Wigan)	penalty	14-10
62 min.	Offiah (Wigan)	try	18-10
	Botica (Wigan)	conversion	20-10
69 min.	Panapa (Wigan)	try	24-10
	Botica (Wigan)	conversion	26-10
77 min.	Cummins (Leeds)	try	26-14
	Holroyd (Leeds)	conversion	26-16

WIGAN v. BRISBANE BRONCOS World Club Challenge
1 June 1994, ANZ Stadium, Brisbane

Wigan completed a trio of World Club Challenge victories with one of their finest ever performances. Defeating Brisbane Broncos on their own soil answered the critics from Down Under who claimed that England's success in the contest (three wins out of four before this match) was due to 'home' advantage and the fact that the Australian Premiers normally journeyed to the Northern Hemisphere at the conclusion of their own energy-draining campaign. This time, Brisbane were in the midst of their domestic season, Wigan playing the game after completing a gruelling 45-match schedule in Britain. Wigan were further disadvantaged by the absence of props Kelvin Skerrett (injured in the previous week's Premiership final against Castleford) and Andy Platt (who withdrew having committed to signing for Auckland Warriors, resulting in him being 'dropped' for the Premiership final).

Wigan took Brisbane by surprise by surging into a 12-0 lead after only 16 minutes, despite the Queensland heat, through tries by Denis Betts (who beat off two defenders in following up a Shaun Edwards overhead kick) and Barrie-Jon Mather (who later dislocated his shoulder) after a break by Phil Clarke. Needless to say, the consistent footwork of Frano Botica added the goal points to both efforts. The only other score of the first period went to Brisbane's wingman Wendell Sailor, who went over in the corner from a play-the-ball.

When Brisbane's other star winger Michael Hancock spilled possession early in the second half, presenting Jason Robinson with an unexpected opportunist try – Botica adding the conversion – Wigan began to look a solid bet with an 18-4 lead.

The Broncos, determined not to be embarrassed further, staged a fightback and put the Wigan defence under tremendous pressure. The fact that only two tries were conceded during this period – by Hancock and Julian O'Neill – is a testimony to Wigan's character. With O'Neill converting his own effort, it left Brisbane only four points behind with a quarter of the match remaining. Somehow, the Wigan line remained intact and, thanks to a Botica penalty in the 66th minute, they even managed to increase the lead before the finish. The result avenged the 22-8 defeat by Brisbane at Central Park in the 1992 Challenge and boosted the Central Park coffers thanks to the 'winner takes all' prize of £200,000.

Martin Offiah, patriotically adorned with a 'Union Jack' flag, holds the World Club Challenge trophy aloft.

Triumphant captain Edwards said after the game: 'We didn't play all that well in attack because the ball was like a bar of soap in the humid conditions but we took our chances and that's what we do in big games.'

Match statistics:
Wigan 20 Brisbane Broncos 14
World Club Challenge
Wednesday 1 June 1994 at ANZ Stadium, Brisbane (kick-off: 7.30 p.m. local time)

Wigan	**Brisbane Broncos**
(cherry and white hoops)	(maroon, white and yellow)

Full-back:	
Gary Connolly	Willie Carne

Three-quarters:	
Jason Robinson (try)	Wendell Sailor (try)
Sam Panapa	Steve Renouf
Barrie-Jon Mather (try)	Chris Johns
Martin Offiah	Michael Hancock (try)

Half-backs:	
Frano Botica (4 goals)	Kevin Walters
Shaun Edwards (captain)	Allan Langer (captain)

Forwards:	
Neil Cowie	Glenn Lazarus
Martin Dermott	Kerrod Walters
Billy McGinty	Andrew Gee
Denis Betts (try)	Mark Hohn
Andy Farrell	Alan Cann
Phil Clarke	Julian O'Neill (try, goal)

Substitutes:	
Martin Hall for Dermott 23 min.	John Plath for Kevin Walters 6 min.
Mick Cassidy for McGinty 26 min.	Peter Ryan for Renouf 23 min.
Paul Atcheson for Mather 50 min.	Brett Galea for Gee 65 min.
Va'aiga Tuigamala (did not play)	Chris McKenna for Plath 74 min.

Caretaker-coach:	*Coach:*
Graeme West	Wayne Bennett

Referee: Greg McCallum (Australia)
Attendance: 54,220
Weather: Very warm and humid

Half-time: 12-4
Receipts: A$448,041

First half:

7 min.	Betts (Wigan)	try	4-0
	Botica (Wigan)	conversion	6-0
16 min.	Mather (Wigan)	try	10-0
	Botica (Wigan)	conversion	12-0
27 min.	Sailor (Brisbane Broncos)	try	12-4

Second half:

42 min.	Robinson (Wigan)	try	16-4
	Botica (Wigan)	conversion	18-4
46 min.	Hancock (Brisbane Broncos)	try	18-8
59 min.	O'Neill (Brisbane Broncos)	try	18-12
	O'Neill (Brisbane Broncos)	conversion	18-14
66 min.	Botica (Wigan)	penalty	20-14

WIGAN v. LEEDS Rugby League Challenge Cup final
29 April 1995, Wembley Stadium, London

Wigan and Leeds made Challenge Cup history in 1995 as the first pair to meet at Wembley in successive finals. For Leeds it was not a happy return, losing more convincingly than twelve months earlier (when the try count had been 4-3 for Wigan), this time conceding five while scoring just one themselves. The eventual 30-10 victory for Wigan was to be the last of their historic – and surely unsurpassable – run of eight consecutive Wembley triumphs, a sequence that incorporated six League and Cup doubles. Leeds entered the fray with some confidence, having beaten Wigan four months earlier in a League fixture, although a shoulder injury going into the match subdued the threat posed by skipper Ellery Hanley.

Leeds' only first-half points came from two Graham Holroyd penalties, the first opening the scoring after three minutes when Kelvin Skerrett was guilty of lying on after a tackle. Just 15 minutes later, Martin Offiah appeared on the right side of the Wigan attack to send Jason Robinson on a 35-yard run into the right corner, shrugging off a Francis Cummins tackle and outwitting three other defenders in the process. Frano Botica added the goal and Wigan led 6-2. Leeds never regained the lead, Henry Paul spinning over for a second try in the 26th minute off a Phil Clarke pass, following a 40-yard burst down the middle from Denis Betts. The half closed with a penalty apiece (both for offside), Holroyd's second effort being matched by Botica.

Any ambitions that Leeds had of eroding Wigan's 12-4 interval lead disappeared when Robinson got his second five minutes after the restart. From acting half-back, he took advantage of poor marking at a play-the-ball in midfield to race through a group of half a dozen defenders (who seemed to freeze) for a sensational try. Wigan added two more during the next 20 minutes. The first by hooker Martin Hall, making his Wembley debut, again capitalised on poor play-the-ball cover as he 'dummied' his way over from acting half-back after Andy Farrell had been held near the try-line. Va'aiga Tuigamala, got the next, the heavyweight centre powering past four opponents on his run in. With Botica converting all three second-half tries, the scoreline accelerated to 30-4. Two minutes from time James Lowes sneaked in for the only Leeds try following a tap penalty ten yards out, Holroyd kicking the goal.

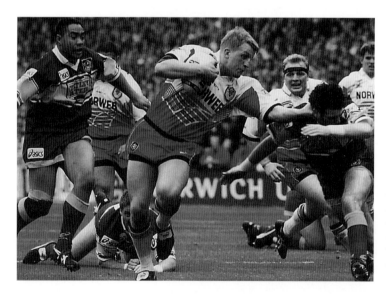

Wigan's Denis Betts tries to force a gap between Leeds forwards Esene Faimalo (left) and Richard Eyres. Wigan hooker Martin Hall (with headband) supports in the background.

WIGAN v. LEEDS

In winning, Wigan showed ruthless efficiency with the pack, ably led by a rampaging performance from props Skerrett and Neil Cowie, who were in control throughout and inflicted Leeds' heaviest Challenge Cup final loss.

Match statistics:
Wigan 30 Leeds 10
Rugby League Challenge Cup final
Saturday 29 April 1995 at Wembley Stadium, London (kick-off: 2.30 p.m.)

Wigan	*Leeds*
(cherry and white hoops)	(blue with amber band)

Full-back:
Henry Paul (try)   Alan Tait

Three-quarters:
Jason Robinson (2 tries)   Jim Fallon
Va'aiga Tuigamala (try)   Kevin Iro
Gary Connolly   Craig Innes
Martin Offiah   Francis Cummins

Half-backs:
Frano Botica (5 goals)   Garry Schofield
Shaun Edwards (captain)   Graham Holroyd (3 goals)

Forwards:
Kelvin Skerrett, Martin Hall (try),   Harvey Howard, James Lowes (try),
Neil Cowie, Denis Betts,   Esene Faimalo, Gary Mercer,
Mick Cassidy, Phil Clarke   Richard Eyres, Ellery Hanley (captain)

Substitutes:
Andy Farrell for Cassidy 5 min.   George Mann for Howard 33 min.
Paul Atcheson for Skerrett 53 min.   Howard for Faimalo 53 min.
Skerrett for Atcheson 73 min.   Neil Harmon for Eyres 58 min.

Coach: *Coach:*
Graeme West   Doug Laughton

Referee: Russell Smith (Castleford)   *Half-time:* 12-4
Attendance: 78,550   *Receipts:* £2,040,000
Weather: Cloudy, dry conditions

First half:
3 min.	Holroyd (Leeds)	penalty	0-2
18 min.	Robinson (Wigan)	try	4-2
	Botica (Wigan)	conversion	6-2
26 min.	Paul (Wigan)	try	10-2
34 min.	Holroyd (Leeds)	penalty	10-4
39 min.	Botica (Wigan)	penalty	12-4

Second half:
45 min.	Robinson (Wigan)	try	16-4
	Botica (Wigan)	conversion	18-4
52 min.	Hall (Wigan)	try	22-4
	Botica (Wigan)	conversion	24-4
65 min.	Tuigamala (Wigan)	try	28-4
	Botica (Wigan)	conversion	30-4
78 min.	Lowes (Leeds)	try	30-8
	Holroyd (Leeds)	conversion	30-10

WIGAN v. LEEDS Premiership Trophy final
21 May 1995, Old Trafford, Manchester

Wigan humiliated their Yorkshire rivals Leeds in registering an emphatic 69-12 victory at Old Trafford in the 1995 Premiership decider. It was the biggest score ever recorded in a Rugby League final for any competition and completed a clean sweep of the season's honours. The match was a sell-out, the attendance of 30,160 being limited due to redevelopment work taking place at Old Trafford.

Fate dealt Wigan a hand when Va'aiga Tuigamala was forced to withdraw to attend a family funeral in New Zealand, opening the way for nineteen-year-old Kris Radlinski to line up at centre. Radlinski, who, along with co-centre Gary Connolly, became the first to score a Premiership final try hat-trick, was to be the youngest ever winner of the Harry Sunderland Man of the Match award. Meanwhile, Leeds were missing two of their most influential players with captain Ellery Hanley being injured and Garry Schofield suspended.

Radlinski opened the scoring after eight minutes following a wonderful attacking move involving five players, Frano Botica adding the conversion as he set about equalling his record of goals (10) and points (20) set in the 1992 final. When Richard Eyres responded with a try six minutes later and Graham Holroyd goaled it to level the scores, it appeared that a keenly fought final was in prospect. The Cherry and Whites quickly dispelled any such thought when Kelvin Skerrett powered over three minutes later, with further first-half tries ensuing from Radlinski, Connolly (two) and Shaun Edwards. The second Connolly effort, in the 32nd minute, was the most spectacular of the match. It began when Jason Robinson spurted away from the Wigan try-line, the ball transferring to Botica and then Henry Paul. Paul, who had a tremendous match at full-back, handed to Connolly, who completed a magical length-of-the-field move that had the crowd on its feet. Botica converted each try for a 36-6 interval lead.

Radlinski completed his try trio within three minutes of the second half kicking off. For once Botica missed the goal, but was on the mark for further tries by Denis

The Leeds player (bottom left) must be wondering what has happened, the scoreboard at the back of the stand telling its own tale. The empty seats to the left were due to redevelopment work at Old Trafford.

Betts and Paul, putting Wigan in a commanding 52-6 lead with 30 minutes still to play! Connolly got his third, which was followed minutes later by a try from hooker Martin Hall before Leeds troubled the scoreboard again when Craig Innes got their second, Holroyd's goal making it 62-12. In the final minutes, Andy Farrell added a drop goal and Simon Haughton a try before Botica's goal completed the scoring.

Match statistics:
Wigan 69 Leeds 12
Premiership Trophy final
Sunday 21 May 1995 at Old Trafford, Manchester (kick-off: 4.00 p.m.)

Wigan	**Leeds**
(cherry and white hoops)	(blue with amber band and sleeves)

Full-back:
Henry Paul (try)   Alan Tait

Three-quarters:
Jason Robinson, Kris Radlinski (3 tries),   Jim Fallon, Kevin Iro (captain),
Gary Connolly (3 tries), Martin Offiah   Phil Hassan, Francis Cummins

Half-backs:
Frano Botica (10 goals)   Craig Innes (try)
Shaun Edwards (captain, try)   Graham Holroyd (2 goals)

Forwards:
Kelvin Skerrett (try), Martin Hall (try),   Harvey Howard, James Lowes,
Neil Cowie, Denis Betts (try),   Esene Faimalo, George Mann,
Andy Farrell (drop goal), Phil Clarke   Richard Eyres (try), Gary Mercer

Substitutes:
Mick Cassidy for Skerrett 20 min.   Neil Harmon for Howard 29 min.
Simon Haughton (try) for Farrell 49 min.   Marcus Vassilakopoulos for Hassan 40 min.
Farrell for Paul 60 min.   Howard for Harmon 53 min.

Coach: *Coach:*
Graeme West   Doug Laughton

Referee: Stuart Cummings (Widnes)   *Half-time:* 36-6
Attendance: 30,160   *Receipts:* £351,038
Weather: Overcast and warm, dry

First half:

8 min.	Radlinski/Botica (Wigan)	try/conversion	6-0
14 min.	Eyres/Holroyd (Leeds)	try/conversion	6-6
17 min.	Skerrett/Botica (Wigan)	try/conversion	12-6
24 min.	Radlinski/Botica (Wigan)	try/conversion	18-6
28 min.	Connolly/Botica (Wigan)	try/conversion	24-6
32 min.	Connolly/Botica (Wigan)	try/conversion	30-6
39 min.	Edwards/Botica (Wigan)	try/conversion	36-6

Second half:

43 min.	Radlinski (Wigan)	try	40-6
47 min.	Betts/Botica (Wigan)	try/conversion	46-6
50 min.	Paul/Botica (Wigan)	try/conversion	52-6
60 min.	Connolly (Wigan)	try	56-6
62 min.	Hall/Botica (Wigan)	try/conversion	62-6
68 min.	Innes/Holroyd (Leeds)	try/conversion	62-12
75 min.	Farrell (Wigan)	drop goal	63-12
76 min.	Haughton/Botica (Wigan)	try/conversion	69-12

WIGAN v. ST HELENS Premiership Trophy final
8 September 1996, Old Trafford, Manchester

This was a match where Wigan captain Andy Farrell, at just twenty-one-years old, came of age, leading his side to a much-needed win over St Helens and earning himself the prestigious Harry Sunderland Trophy as Man of the Match in the process. As Wigan anticipated their final match of the first summer Super League season, they faced the prospect of being trophyless for the first time since the 1983/84 campaign. Rivals St Helens had added to their Challenge Cup success that season by edging Wigan out of the Super League title by one point (thereby ending a run of seven consecutive championships) and were chasing a treble.

The manner and margin of Wigan's victory was unexpected, many critics already writing the side off as past their peak. The Cherry and Whites gave St Helens an early warning of what was in store when Gary Connolly covered 30 yards before touching down in the tenth minute, despite the attention of Saints full-back Steve Prescott. A classic confrontation looked a possibility when Paul Newlove powered his way past two defenders to score four minutes later, Bobbie Goulding's conversion putting the Knowsley Road men ahead 6-4. The pendulum swung back to Wigan when Jason Robinson – who had an outstanding game – ripped through the Saints' defence to set up Shaun Edwards, Farrell adding the goal. Before the break, Danny Ellison added two more (unconverted) tries, Goulding scoring from a penalty for St Helens, giving Wigan an 18-8 interval lead.

In the opening period of the second half St Helens had their best spell of the final and when Newlove beat off two would-be tackles to send Tommy Martyn over eight minutes after the resumption it appeared that they were well and truly back in the contest. Goulding's goal put Saints within striking distance at 18-14, but that was to be the last time they troubled the scoreboard.

In a repeat performance of the 1992 Premiership final between the two, Wigan cut loose in the final 30 minutes with five sizzling tries. Farrell had a hand in the first two – scored by Simon Haughton and Henry Paul – before Robinson went in after one of his typical weaving runs. Craig Murdock (almost with his first touch of the ball after replacing Edwards) and Ellison (completing his hat-trick) added the others. Farrell, whose one flaw in a brilliant display was that he appeared to have left his kicking boots in the locker, converted three of his side's second-half tries to round off the scoring.

Gary Connolly has Henry Paul (left) in support as he looks to evade Saints' Keiron Cunningham (9).

Match statistics:
Wigan 44 St Helens 14
Premiership Trophy final
Sunday 8 September 1996 at Old Trafford, Manchester (kick-off: 7.00 p.m.)

Wigan	**St Helens**
(blue and white chequered)	(red and white)

Full-back:
Kris Radlinski   Steve Prescott

Three-quarters:
Danny Ellison (3 tries), Gary Connolly (try),   Joe Hayes, Alan Hunte,
Va'aiga Tuigamala, Jason Robinson (try)   Paul Newlove (try), Anthony Sullivan

Half-backs:
Henry Paul (try)   Tommy Martyn (try)
Shaun Edwards (try)   Bobbie Goulding (captain, 3 goals)

Forwards:
Kelvin Skerrett, Martin Hall,   Apollo Perelini, Keiron Cunningham,
Terry O'Connor, Simon Haughton (try),   Adam Fogerty, Derek McVey,
Mick Cassidy, Andy Farrell   Chris Morley, Karle Hammond
(captain, 4 goals)

Substitutes:
Neil Cowie for Skerrett 30 min.   Ian Pickavance for Fogerty 25 min.
Steve Barrow for Haughton 62 min.   Danny Arnold for Hayes 64 min.
Skerrett for O'Connor 62 min.   Andy Haigh for Morley 64 min.
Andrew Johnson for Cassidy 67 min.   Simon Booth for McVey 69 min.
Craig Murdock (try) for Edwards 72 min.   Fogerty for Perelini 69 min.
O'Connor for Cowie 78 min.   Hayes for Newlove 71 min.

Coach: *Coach:*
Graeme West   Shaun McRae

Referee: David Campbell (Widnes)   *Half-time:* 18-8
Attendance: 35,013   *Receipts:* £404,000
Weather: Cloudy, slight breeze

First half:

10 min.	Connolly (Wigan)	try	4-0
14 min.	Newlove (St Helens)	try	4-4
	Goulding (St Helens)	conversion	4-6
22 min.	Edwards (Wigan)	try	8-6
	Farrell (Wigan)	conversion	10-6
26 min.	Ellison (Wigan)	try	14-6
30 min.	Goulding (St Helens)	penalty	14-8
36 min.	Ellison (Wigan)	try	18-8

Second half:

48 min.	Martyn (St Helens)	try	18-12
	Goulding (St Helens)	conversion	18-14
51 min.	Haughton (Wigan)	try	22-14
63 min.	Paul (Wigan)	try	26-14
	Farrell (Wigan)	conversion	28-14
67 min.	Robinson (Wigan)	try	32-14
	Farrell (Wigan)	conversion	34-14
77 min.	Murdock (Wigan)	try	38-14
	Farrell (Wigan)	conversion	40-14
79 min.	Ellison (Wigan)	try	44-14

WIGAN WARRIORS v. ST HELENS Premiership Trophy final
28 September 1997, Old Trafford, Manchester

Wigan – known as the Warriors from the 1997 season – appeared in their sixth consecutive Premiership Trophy final, meeting St Helens for the fourth time during that sequence. It was also Wigan's fourth successive win in the final – a competition record – in what would be the last contest for the Premiership Trophy (replaced by the Grand Final from 1998). Skipper Andy Farrell repeated his success of the previous year by again taking the Harry Sunderland Trophy, receiving twenty-six of the twenty-eight votes from the members of the Rugby League Writers' Association present.

The first half saw the teams each register two tries with Farrell being the provider for both Wigan efforts with two perfectly placed kicks for Andy Johnson (four minutes) and Jason Robinson (31 minutes) to connect with. Derek McVey (put through by Sean Long on 23 minutes) and Paul Newlove (from a well-timed Keiron Cunningham pass after 34) scored the St Helens tries, Farrell's three goals (two penalties and one conversion) making the difference when the teams returned to the changing rooms at the break, Wigan leading 14-8.

A penalty from Long two minutes after the restart brought St Helens to within four points of Wigan but, as in previous Premiership finals, the Warriors lifted the tempo, adding nineteen points during a twenty-minute assault on the Saints' defence. Farrell led off with a penalty in the 44th minute, substitute Nigel Wright succeeding with a drop goal three minutes later. It was at this stage, with the score at 17-10, that Robinson pulled off a superb tackle on Anthony Sullivan, who had looked odds-on to bring his side back into contention after racing half the length of the field. With that crisis dealt with, Wigan grabbed the first of their three second-half tries, Kris Radlinski taking advantage of an overlap worked by Farrell and Simon Haughton. Farrell himself got the next after a length-of-the-field move and, finally,

Haughton got on the scoreboard, Farrell once more playing a part in the build-up. Farrell added two of the goals, giving Wigan a commanding 33-10 lead. With only four minutes remaining St Helens boosted their score with tries from Paul Anderson (converted by Long) and Karle Hammond. Those late scores put the final try-count at 5-4 in Wigan's favour, numbers that did not reflect the Warriors' overall superiority.

Wigan coach Eric Hughes, who had replaced Graeme West at the start of the season, found the result personally satisfying, as the win was against the club that had dismissed him the previous year.

Captain and Harry Sunderland Trophy winner Andy Farrell weighed in with a try and six goals.

Match statistics:
Wigan Warriors 33 St Helens 20
Premiership Trophy final
Sunday 28 September 1997 at Old Trafford, Manchester (kick-off: 3.00 p.m.)

Wigan Warriors	*St Helens*
(blue and pale blue)	(red, black and white)

Full-back:
Jason Robinson (try)   Danny Arnold

Three-quarters:
Andy Johnson (try)	Anthony Stewart
Kris Radlinski (try)	Alan Hunte
Gary Connolly	Paul Newlove (try)
Danny Ellison	Anthony Sullivan

Half-backs:
| Henry Paul | Karle Hammond (try) |
| Tony Smith | Sean Long (2 goals) |

Forwards:
Neil Cowie, Jon Clarke, Lee Hansen, Simon Haughton (try), Mick Cassidy, Andy Farrell (captain, try, 6 goals)

Andy Leathem, Keiron Cunningham, Julian O'Neill, Apollo Perelini, Derek McVey (try), Chris Joynt (captain)

Substitutes:
Nigel Wright (drop goal) for Connolly 25 min.
Terry O'Connor for Cowie 25 min.
Stephen Holgate for Hansen 45 min.
Gael Tallec for Smith 50 min.
Cowie for O'Connor 58 min.

Simon Booth for O'Neill 53 min.
Ian Pickavance for Leathem 53 min.
Chris Morley for Perelini 60 min.
Paul Anderson (try) for McVey 65 min.

Blood-bin replacements:
Wright for Smith 2-14 min.
Tallec for Smith 36-37 min.

Pickavance for O'Neill 19-40 min.

Coach: *Coach:*
Eric Hughes   Shaun McRae

Referee: Stuart Cummings (Widnes)   *Half-time:* 14-8
Attendance: 33,389   *Receipts:* £359,303
Weather: Sunny and mild

First half:

4 min.	Johnson (Wigan)	try	4-0
8 min.	Farrell (Wigan)	penalty	6-0
23 min.	McVey (St Helens)	try	6-4
26 min.	Farrell (Wigan)	penalty	8-4
31 min.	Robinson/Farrell (Wigan)	try/conversion	14-4
34 min.	Newlove (St Helens)	try	14-8

Second half:

42 min.	Long (St Helens)	penalty	14-10
44 min.	Farrell (Wigan)	penalty	16-10
47 min.	Wright (Wigan)	drop goal	17-10
52 min.	Radlinski/Farrell (Wigan)	try/conversion	23-10
59 min.	Farrell (Wigan)	try	27-10
64 min.	Haughton/Farrell (Wigan)	try/conversion	33-10
76 min.	Anderson/Long (St Helens)	try/conversion	33-16
79 min.	Hammond (St Helens)	try	33-20

WIGAN WARRIORS v. LEEDS RHINOS Super League Grand Final
24 October 1998, Old Trafford, Manchester

Wigan featured in the first ever Super League Grand Final when they took on Leeds in a bruising encounter at Old Trafford, the outcome of which was not resolved until the end of the evening. The decision to adopt the Australian-style top-five play-off system had been a controversial one, but the attendance – 43,553 on a very wet and windy evening – exceeded the best for a Premiership final, the competition that it had effectively replaced. The receipts also provided a record for a match staged outside of Wembley. Whereas the Premiership had been a competition in its own right, the Grand Final determined the destination of the third Super League title, the previous two having gone to the side topping the League table.

For long periods during the first half, the Leeds Rhinos (who had finished second in the League to Wigan) looked the more likely side to take the title, Iestyn Harris in particular proving a constant threat to the Wigan defence. Their only reward was a try by Ritchie Blackmore, who took a well-timed pass from Ryan Sheridan mid-way through the first half. This put Leeds 4-0 in front, their only points of the match. With the interval approaching, Jason Robinson – unexpectedly and against the general run of play at the time – provided the key moment of the night with a brilliant solo effort. In a move that ultimately determined the destination of the trophy, he ran from acting half-back at a play-the-ball, evading the clutches of several defenders as he sped away to cross the try-line. Andy Farrell's goal pushed the Warriors into an unexpected 6-4 lead at the break.

Possibly as a result of the Robinson score, the momentum switched to Wigan in the second half, Leeds not helping their cause with several handling errors in the wet conditions. Wigan, inspired by an excellent all-round performance from Farrell, who later admitted it was 'as tough a game as I have played in', showed greater intensity as the match wore on. The only points scored after the interval, during a half that developed into a real battle of attrition, were two penalties from the Wigan captain. The second of those, a minute from the end, effectively made the game safe for the Warriors.

Robinson's gem gives Wigan winning feeling

Jason Robinson's vital try received full credit from the pen of Dave Hadfield in *The Independent*.

WIGAN WARRIORS v. LEEDS RHINOS

The result provided Wigan's only silverware of the season as they extended their remarkable record of trophy-collecting to fifteen consecutive seasons. Equally welcome was the record £275,000 winners' purse, runners-up Leeds doing very nicely with a 'consolation' cheque of £175,000!

Match statistics:
Wigan Warriors 10 Leeds Rhinos 4
Super League Grand Final
Saturday 24 October 1998 at Old Trafford, Manchester (kick-off: 6.30 p.m.)

Wigan Warriors	*Leeds Rhinos*
(cherry and white)	(blue and amber)

Full-back:
Kris Radlinski   Iestyn Harris (captain)

Three-quarters:
Jason Robinson (try), Danny Moore,   Leroy Rivett, Richard Blackmore (try),
Gary Connolly, Mark Bell   Brad Godden, Francis Cummins

Half-backs:
Henry Paul, Tony Smith   Daryl Powell, Ryan Sheridan

Forwards:
Terry O'Connor, Robbie McCormack,   Martin Masella, Terry Newton,
Tony Mestrov, Lee Gilmour,   Darren Fleary, Adrian Morley,
Stephen Holgate, Andy Farrell   Anthony Farrell, Marc Glanville
(captain, 3 goals)

Substitutes:
Simon Haughton for Holgate 33 min.   Jamie Mathiou for Masella 25 min.
Paul Johnson for Moore 37 min.   Marcus St Hilaire for Powell 40 min.
Neil Cowie for Mestrov 54 min.   Graham Holroyd for Newton 49 min.
Mick Cassidy for Haughton 64 min.   Andy Hay for Fleary 54 min.
Holgate for Cowie 68 min.   Powell for Godden 58 min.
                                                                    Masella for Mathiou 71 min.

Blood-bin replacements:
Cowie for O'Connor 18-48 min.
Cassidy for McCormack 19-27 min.
Haughton for Gilmour 27-33 min.
Haughton for Gilmour 71-75 min.
Mestrov for O'Connor 75 min.

Coach: *Coach:*
John Monie   Graham Murray

Referee: Russell Smith (Castleford)   *Half-time:* 6-4
Attendance: 43,553   *Receipts:* £637,105
Weather: Heavy rain, blustery winds

First half:

21 min.	Blackmore (Leeds)	try	0-4
38 min.	Robinson (Wigan)	try	4-4
	Farrell (Wigan)	conversion	6-4

Second half:

47 min.	Farrell (Wigan)	penalty	8-4
79 min.	Farrell (Wigan)	penalty	10-4

WIGAN WARRIORS v. ST HELENS Rugby League Challenge Cup final
27 April 2002, Murrayfield, Edinburgh

The 2002 Challenge Cup final against pre-match favourites St Helens, played in Edinburgh, will forever be associated with Wigan full-back Kris Radlinski, whose heroic performance earned him the Lance Todd Trophy. Hospitalised the week before the final with a badly swollen foot – believed to be the result of an insect bite – he was declared fit by the club doctor 90 minutes before kick-off. If Radlinski held any fears of breaking down during the match, it did not show, his commitment in both attack and defence inspiring a magnificent victory.

Radlinski made an early try-saving tackle on Tim Jonkers before Wigan raced in for two tries in five minutes from Brett Dallas (in the right corner after a superb attacking move instigated by Radlinski, who offloaded the ball in a two-man tackle) and Adrian Lam (sidestepping two defenders after taking an inside pass from David Furner). With Andy Farrell adding both goals it gave Wigan an early and confidence-boosting 12-0 cushion. St Helens put their game together, and in the 22nd minute Darren Albert got their opening try, outjumping Jamie Ainscough on the line to collect a perfectly judged Sean Long kick into the corner. Radlinski then saved a certain score on 25 minutes (a controversial decision by the video referee) when the Wigan full-back appeared to get his foot under the ball as Keiron Cunningham attempted to touch down under the posts. St Helens were looking the stronger side and, from a play-the-ball just two yards from the try-line, the ball was passed quickly to the right, Martin Gleeson evading two defenders to score after 31 minutes. With Long failing to convert the two St Helens efforts, half-time arrived with Wigan 12-8 in front.

St Helens continued to press in the second half, Paul Sculthorpe having a try disallowed when Gleeson was penalised for not playing a play-the-ball correctly in the build-up. Farrell's relieving penalty kick to touch swung the momentum back to Wigan, a Julian O'Neill break ending with Gary Connolly being the recipient of a try-scoring Paul Johnson pass a minute later. Farrell's conversion made it 18-8. Sculthorpe eventually scored for Saints on the hour, Long missing the goal with his easiest chance so far. St Helens again looked dangerous, and Radlinski pulled off another superb try-line tackle on Jonkers. Farrell ended the threat with a 40/20 kick to touch, with Lam on target with a drop goal after Farrell was held inches short. Farrell concluded the scoring with a penalty five minutes from time when Terry Newton had the ball ripped out while attempting to score.

Kris Radlinski surveys his badly swollen foot the day before his Lance Todd winning performance.

Match statistics:
Wigan Warriors 21 St Helens 12
Rugby League Challenge Cup final
Saturday 27 April 2002 at Murrayfield, Edinburgh (kick-off: 2.45 p.m.)

Wigan Warriors	**St Helens**
(dark blue)	(red and white)

Full-back:
| Kris Radlinski | Paul Wellens |

Three-quarters:
Brett Dallas (try)	Darren Albert (try)
Gary Connolly (try)	Martin Gleeson (try)
Jamie Ainscough	Paul Newlove
Paul Johnson	Anthony Stewart

Half-backs:
| Julian O'Neill | Tommy Martyn |
| Adrian Lam (try, drop goal) | Sean Long |

Forwards:
Terry O'Connor	Darren Britt
Terry Newton	Keiron Cunningham
Craig Smith	Peter Shiels
Mick Cassidy	Chris Joynt (captain)
David Furner	Tim Jonkers
Andy Farrell (captain, 4 goals)	Paul Sculthorpe (try)

Substitutes:
Ricky Bibey for C Smith 32 min.	John Stankevitch for Britt 32 min.
David Hodgson for Cassidy 41 min.	Sean Hoppe for Joynt 56 min.
C Smith for O'Connor 51 min.	Britt for Stankevitch 56 min.
Mark Smith for Furner 64 min.	Britt for Hopped 67 min.
O'Connor for C Smith 67 min.	Barry Ward for Shiels 70 min.
C Smith for Carney 72 min.	Mick Higham for Jonkers 77 min.

Blood-bin replacements:
Brian Carney for Dallas 64 min.	Ward for Shiels 31-49 min.
Dallas for Bibey 71 min.	Joynt for Britt 65 min.
Carney for Newton 77 min.	Shiels for Britt 75 min.

Coach:
| Stuart Raper | Ian Millward |

Referee: Stuart Cummings (Widnes)
Attendance: 62,140
Weather: Sunny, some cloud, very warm

Half-time: 12-8

First half:

11 min.	Dallas (Wigan)	try	4-0
	Farrell (Wigan)	conversion	6-0
15 min.	Lam (Wigan)	try	10-0
	Farrell (Wigan)	conversion	12-0
22 min.	Albert (St Helens)	try	12-4
31 min.	Gleeson (St Helens)	try	12-8

Second half:

51 min.	Connolly (Wigan)	try	16-8
	Farrell (Wigan)	conversion	18-8
60 min.	Sculthorpe (St Helens)	try	18-12
66 min.	Lam (Wigan)	drop goal	19-12
76 min.	Farrell (Wigan)	penalty	21-12

Other local interest titles published by Tempus

Wigan Rugby League Football Club
GRAHAM MORRIS

Wigan Rugby League is arguably the most famous name in the history of the sport. Graham Morris and John Riding recount 130 years of deeds and valour, concluding with the era of Super League and summer rugby, as the renamed Wigan Warriors seek to add to their impressive trophy haul in the magnificent setting of the new all-seater JJB stadium.
0 7524 2299 5

Rugby League Hall of Fame
ROBERT GATE

The Rugby League Hall of Fame was established in 1988 to celebrate the playing legends that have lit up the sport over the decades. This book, which includes Wigan greats Billy Boston and Jim Sullivan, celebrates these mighty heroes of the game and features a detailed personal and playing biography for each of them.
0 7524 2693 1

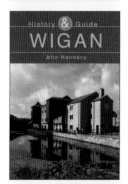

Wigan History & Guide
JOHN HANNAVY

Today, Wigan is a lively mixture of old and new, with Wigan Pier becoming one of the country's most successful tourist attractions, as well as one of the most inspired examples of industrial restoration. This book includes two walking tours of the town which can be used independently of the main text and enable readers to explore the history of Wigan through the streets, buildings and monuments that can still be found there today.
0 7524 3099 8

The Wigan Coalfield
ALAN DAVIES

Through documents, the Wigan area can trace its coal-mining activities as far back as 650 years, and for a brief spell in the late nineteenth century Wigan itself was proudly known as 'Coalopolis'. This is a book that will provide an intriguing insight into the lives and working conditions of Wigan area miners, and is a testament to the region and its proud coal-mining legacy.
0 7524 1724 X

If you are interested in purchasing other books published by Tempus, or in case you have difficulty finding any Tempus books in your local bookshop, you can also place orders directly through our website
www.tempus-publishing.com